Preaching To A Church In Crisis

A Homiletic For
The Last Days Of
The Mainline Church

John Killinger

CSS Publishing Company, Inc.
Lima, Ohio

Copyright © 1995 by
CSS Publishing Company, Inc.
Lima, Ohio

Scripture quotations are from the *Revised Standard Version of the Bible,* copyright-ed 1946, 1952 (c), 1971, 1973, by the Division of Christian Education of the National Council of the Churches of Christ in the USA. Used by permission.

Library of Congress Cataloging-in-Publication Data

Killinger, John.
    Preaching to a church in crisis : the last days of the mainline church / John Killinger.
       p.   cm.
    Includes bibliographical references.
    ISBN 0-7880-0308-9
    1. Church renewal. 2. Protestant churches — United States — 20th century. 3. United States — Church history — 20th century. 4. Christianity and culture. I. Title.
BV600.2.K47   1995
280'.4'097309049—dc20
                                       94-38058
                                            CIP

This book is available in the following formats, listed by ISBN:
0-7880-0308-9 Book
0-7880-0309-7 IBM 3 1/2 computer disk
0-7880-0310-0 IBM 3 1/2 book and disk package
0-7880-0311-9 Macintosh computer disk
0-7880-0312-7 Macintosh book and disk package
0-7880-0313-5 IBM 5 1/4 computer disk
0-7880-0314-3 IBM 5 1/4 book and disk package

PRINTED IN U.S.A.

*For the thousands of
faithful ministers and chaplains
whose love and friendship
have sustained me
across the years:*

*I hope you know
you are God's angels!*

Table Of Contents

Introduction

A few years ago, when our two sons were in their early teens, they were visited by their favorite female cousin. On one inclement day during the visit, the three of them decided to play Blind Man's Bluff, the game in which one player leaves the room, dons a blindfold, and returns to search for the other players, who have meanwhile hidden themselves somewhere in the room. Caught up in the excitement of the game, our sons devised a plan for baffling their cousin: while she was out of the room they quickly shifted the furniture about, so that the room she reentered was entirely different from the one she left. After several minutes of stumbling about and bumping into furniture in the "wrong" places, she became utterly desperate and collapsed to the floor in tears.

There are not a few of us who feel this way about life itself today. Since we entered the game, everything around us has been shifted. Nothing seems to be what it was, or, putting it the other way around, is what it seemed to be. Values have changed, gender roles have altered, commerce has been transmogrified, communications have exploded into something almost entirely new and different, politics have undergone radical transformation, and even the Soviet Union, our old nemesis, has dissolved, leaving us with frightening nuclear arsenals for which there are no real targets. Children in nursery school are now trained on computers, people over 50 have trouble finding new jobs, the drug problem is like a gigantic squid with a stranglehold on civilization itself, most inner cities have become arenas of crime and warfare, the business world has turned into an almost impenetrable tangle of conglomerate management and mismanagement, government is so bureaucratic and unresponsive that not even Don Quixote would seriously undertake to reform it, health care has become a major factor in public planning, the rain forests are being depleted, and 50 percent of the fish being sold in fish markets and supermarkets has bacteria levels 20 times beyond national standards. There is one divorce for every two marriages, more than 50 percent of America's children live in single-parent homes, 80 percent of our teenagers have had sex by the time they graduate from high school, one out of every two fetuses is aborted, the national debt is beyond all personal comprehension, the ozone layer is being eroded even faster than scientists had estimated, and the incidence of melanoma cancer, possibly related to the erosion, is up almost 50 percent in the last five years.

The words of Anthony Newley's song in the hit play of the same name more than 30 years ago were unwittingly prescient: "Stop the world, I want to get off!"

It is hardly surprising that similarly baffling changes have occurred over the last few decades to life and work in the church, which after all is related to the world around it in a symbiosis that only such anachronistic groups as the Amish and Zen Buddhists have been able to defy, and then only with partial (and sometimes enviable) success. The people of the church, after all, adapt to life in computerland, mallworld, and the global village. They talk about megabytes and CDs and triglycerides, and ride the Concorde, visit Epcot Center, and invest in Pacific Rim mutual funds. But neither is it entirely surprising that many people are most upset and even bitter at alterations on the church scene, for churches, especially the churches we have always attended, are the last places in the world we expect to be touched by the winds of change or the acids of modernity. For some reason, we expect our churches, like our favorite grandmothers and perennial vacation spots, to remain forever the same, inviolate and comforting, granitic and reassuring. There is clearly something wrong with the universe — maybe even with God and the old theology — when quiet old sanctuaries and solid old doctrinal sermons give way to rock-and-roll liturgies, psychological pep talks, and group discussions!

Agitation among church members takes many forms. Some merely reminisce about the "good old days" when families sat together for worship, people rarely went out of town on weekends, everybody knew the old hymns, and nobody could remember how many years the present organist and minister had been fixtures in the community. Others openly deplore the modernization of the sanctuary, the newfangled ideas of the pastor, the astronomical size of the budget, and the youth group's discussion of such controversial topics as race, sex, and women in the ministry. All freely admit that the modern church has lost something in translation, and most would suggest that it resembles the pointer on a weathervane more than it does the standard identifying true north.

Ministers in the same churches, if they are over 50, tend to shake their heads and agree with Lyle Schaller, who says, "It is a different world today, and it is far more difficult to be a pastor in today's world than it was as recently as the 1950s."[1] The stresses on the clergy, who are now expected to be Lee Iacocca in the board room, Dr. Joyce Brothers in the counseling session, the Fuller Brush man at house calls, and a combination of Chevy Chase, Tom Brokaw, and Robert Schuller in the pulpit, have grown to be almost unbearable, and the incidence of clergy breakdowns, resignations, scandals, and firings has risen dramatically in recent years.

As a person who has traveled widely and known many ministers in various denominations and church settings, I am often grieved by a phone call or letter from some friend who says, "I have stood it as long as I can. I have given this church my best shot, and it has not worked. I no longer know what to say to these people, or have any confidence that they could hear it if I did. I will not continue to put my family and myself through this kind of hell. I have decided to resign next Sunday, even though I have no place to go.''

Often, those who call or write are among the finest ministers in the U.S., educated at the best schools, articulate in their preaching and writing, imaginative in their attempts at leadership, and deeply committed to Christ and the ministry. They have indeed done their best, often at considerable sacrifice not only to themselves but to their families. The intelligence, training, devotion, and effort they have brought to their work should have spelled resounding success, and probably would have, had it been invested in any other period of history.

But something has happened in our time, or is in the process of happening, that has made the ministry an extremely difficult and precarious place to be. Whatever it is has made churches different, altered the nature of congregational life, introduced disagreement into the question of what it means to live as a Christian, changed people's understandings of the minister's responsibilities, and tended to revise even the consensus of opinion about what constitutes Christian mission, teaching, and preaching.

This book is my attempt to say something to the friends who have called or written about their troubles in ministry, or who may be about to call or write, and to say it from the perspective where I can probably offer the most understanding, namely, what it is like to preach in times like these. After approximately ten years in two major parishes, I have spent the last five years in an academic environment, where I have had the opportunity to catch up on a lot of the material being written about the church today, to reflect on my own experiences with the church (many of which were as difficult and depressing as those of my friends), and to try to wrestle all the ideas and impressions into some sort of meaningful whole. And in the end, because my life has been tied up with preaching, both as a homiletician and as a local pastor, I have tried to ask what the changes in society and the church mean for the way we attempt to proclaim the gospel.

Even the term "proclaim the gospel," I admit, sounds a little strange to my ear now. Perhaps it does to yours. My wife and I were recently talking — maybe dreaming is a better word — about what it would be like to return to life in the pastorate. Suddenly she stunned me with a question: "What would you have to say now?" I merely looked at her. "I mean," she pursued, "what would your message be?" I understood her the first time. I had paused because it was a hard question to answer, or, at least, to answer in a few words. My mind was racing back to the first years of preaching. It had all seemed so simple then. I preached "Jesus Christ, and him crucified," as Paul put it in his letter to the Corinthians. Now, I wasn't sure. Somehow, I knew, I would still preach Jesus. But not as simply and naively as I did then. At least, not to the congregations I would be likely to pastor now. They wouldn't understand such a simple declaration. And I, moreover, would want to qualify what I meant by "Jesus Christ, and him crucified." Either life has become enormously more complicated since I began to preach or my way of understanding things has become more complicated.

I believe I knew what was in my wife's mind when she asked the question. She was thinking about our church experiences and how they had probably affected my attitude about life in the church. Many of the experiences were good. There were moments of beauty and heroism and redemption, occasions of rare and wonderful fellowship, glimpses of the reign of God, times when worship seemed to break through all earthly bounds into regions of heavenly rapture. But there were also times of cruelty and barbarity, when people said or did things that seemed unbelievable in the context of a supposedly redeemed fellowship, when they were petty and mean and vindictive and hurtful. There was the matter of the chipped bowl.

My Los Angeles pastorate was hard, exciting, creative, and impossible. The church had fewer than a third of the members they had said they had. It was awash in a changing neighborhood, and the church's old bluebloods wouldn't give anybody else a paddle. They were determined to preserve themselves as a classical old Anglo congregation in a county that was now 42 percent Hispanic, 20 percent African-American, 20 percent Asian, and only 18 percent Caucasian. We struggled heroically, gradually effecting some changes and instituting service arms that reached out to the poor, illiterate, and homeless of the area. On the whole, it was a very successful ministry. Attendance rose, new people joined, giving increased, involvement grew, long-range planning was undertaken, everything seemed progressive and forward-looking — until I resigned. Then some of the meaner, more contumacious folks began to find the courage to berate the pastor and his wife. One attorney pretty well ruined a gala celebrating our church's citywide Bach festival by buttonholing me and loudly castigating me in front of the crowd for more than an hour. He said I didn't have any vision. I had suggested in a Pentecost sermon that the time might come when the congregation would wish to give the church property to one of the burgeoning Korean congregations in the area. That wasn't the vision he wanted in a minister.

The president of the Women's Association had walked out of church that morning — right in the middle of the sermon. She and the attorney and a handful of others attempted to start a coup that would send me packing before I intended to leave. I learned about it, exposed them at the church's annual meeting, received a standing ovation from the rest of the crowd, and left the coup in a shambles. But when the Board of Trustees (of which the attorney was a prominent member!) and the Women's Association presented us with gifts as we were leaving, we got our comeuppance. The last senior minister and his wife had been given $10,000 to make a trip around the world. The Women's Association had presented the wives of other exiting staff members pearls, necklaces, and expensive wristwatches. I received a watercolor of the church and my wife got a chipped bowl.

We suspected that the bowl had come from the church's thrift shop. But how to confirm it? We didn't discover the chip until we moved away. Then my wife did what any sweet, charming, and completely catty female would do. She wrote the new president of the Women's Association a warmly gracious note of thanks to be read to the entire Association. But, horror of horrors, she added, the merchant who had sold the Association the bowl had given them one with an imperfection. She knew the ladies would not wish her to keep this particular bowl. If they would only send her the name of the merchant, she herself would write and exchange it. The poor president, who is a dear woman and had nothing to do with the selection of the gift, was forced to come clean. The bowl, she wrote, had come from "the valued estate" of a "dear church member," and alas could not be returned. Perhaps it could be mended. My wife did not tell her that when she took the bowl to a shop to ask about having it mended she was told it was worth less than the mending would cost.

My wife knew, when she asked what I would preach now, that such experiences make a difference in the minister's mindset, that, cumulatively, they mature and sharpen and even reorient one's thinking, so that one no longer even looks at church and ministry and preaching in the way they were once envisioned.

I narrate this somewhat pathetic little story merely to assure my readers that I understand what parish life is often like for them today, that it is not the grand and glorious affair it once was (or is thought to have been), when churches were among the nation's most influential institutions, congregations eagerly crowded into sanctuaries to hear their ministers' deeply thought and well-crafted sermons, everyone expressed gratitude for the ministers' presence and talents, and summaries, if not the entirety, of their sermons appeared prominently in community newspapers the following day, but it is now often trifling, mean, and inglorious, or at least tedious and boring and inconsequential.

The title of the book is meant to underline the uniqueness of the present situation, and perhaps the urgency of it, but not to sensationalize it. I think one of the reasons for the troubles we are experiencing, probably the primary reason, is that we are passing through a terrible crisis in the life of the mainline churches. And, inasmuch as the mainline churches for so many years established the social and political norms in our country, as well as the spiritual norms, any crisis in their existence becomes a major crisis in modern Christendom, and, by extension, in American life as a whole.

What I have attempted to do, therefore, is to establish in the opening chapters of the book a general understanding of the malaise now affecting our churches, and then to extrapolate from that understanding a sense of the moods and feelings affecting most of the people in our congregations. If the mainline church is disintegrating as the most formative influence in the American way of life, and the American way itself is in upheaval and flux, what must this do to the psyches of the various persons attending our services, sitting on our boards, and generally determining the futures of our congregations? They are certainly not the same persons their fathers and mothers were, or even the same persons they themselves were 25 years ago. Then, having established an answer to this important question, even partially and tentatively, we shall be in a better position for thinking about our preaching and what its hallmarks must be in order to speak truly and effectively for the gospel in our time.

I don't think it is tipping my hand to say that preachers have not faced such challenges, or lived in such a tumultuous era, since the days of the Reformation itself, when a similar series of shocks and stresses occurred in the history and culture of the world. Then, a revolution of far-reaching and deeply felt consequences produced radical changes in the life of the church and in the way many preachers came to understand their calling and their craft. We may well be in the midst of such a transformation in our own day, and will do well to recognize it. The fundamentalist and traditionalist voices attempting to reinforce the dogmas and emphases of an earlier age, sincere and faithful as they may be, do no service to the church or the world at this point in what is transpiring. They are like similar voices in the sixteenth century that tried to hold back the dam when the modern age was about to burst forth. It is time for us to recognize the enormous changes taking place and, with the boldness born of a new faith and vision, to make some radical adjustments in how we live and speak.

---

1. Lyle Schaller, *It's A Different World!* (Nashville: Abingdon Press, 1987), p. 18.

Chapter 1

The End Of An Era —
And The End Of Mainline?

P.D. James, the British novelist, sets her story *Devices and Desires* in a fictional town called Larksoken on the northeast coast of England. Larksoken is the site of a nuclear power station. James' favorite character, detective Adam Dagliesh, has come to Larksoken to visit his aunt. One evening he attends a dinner party, and afterwards walks home with Meg Dennison. North of them, as their eyes sweep the headland, stands the power station, decked in lights, "its stark geometric bulk subsumed in the blue-black of the sky."

Meg confesses that when she first moved there from London it rather frightened her, out of its sheer size and the way it appeared to dominate the headland. Dagliesh agrees. He would prefer the headland without it, he says, but supposes it is beginning to look as if it has "a right to be there."

"They turned simultaneously from contemplating the glittering lights," says Mrs. James, "and looked south to the decaying symbol of a very different power. Before them, at the edge of the cliff, crumbling against the skyline like a child's sand castle rendered amorphous by the advancing tide, was the ruined Benedictine abbey. He could just make out the great empty arch of the east window and beyond it the shimmer of the North Sea, while above, seeming to move through and over it like a censer, swung the smudged yellow disc of the moon."[1]

There, cryptically and eloquently, stand the twin symbols of Mrs. James' landscape, the great funnels of the nuclear power station and the broken walls of the ancient church. They preside over the entire novel, and, in a sense, over all of Mrs. James' fiction. They are a statement about life in our time. This is the nuclear age, the age of atomic power. The church has had its day and is no more. Its walls are breached, its roofs collapsed.

The aptness of this fictional comment is readily apparent. Fewer than two percent of the populace of Great Britain, we are told, now attend church. The average Sunday attendance in the parishes of the Church of England is less than 20 persons. As the well-known evangelical David Watson wrote in his book *I Believe in the Church,* "the popular image of the church [in England] is that of empty and decaying buildings, aged and female congregations, and depressed and irrelevant clergy."[2]

Watson cites at some length the observations of journalist Malcolm Muggeridge:

> *In an average English village today Anglican worship has become little more than a dying bourgeois cult. A small cluster of motor-cars may be seen outside the parish church when a service is in progress; the bells still ring joyously across the fields and meadows on Sunday mornings and evenings, but fewer and fewer heed them, and those few predominantly middle-class, female and elderly .... It must be desperately disheartening, and the incumbent often gives the impression of being dispirited and forlorn. Whatever zeal he may have had as an ordinand soon gets dissipated in an atmosphere of domestic care and indifference on the part of his flock. Small wonder,*

then, that in the pulpit he has little to say except to repeat the old traditional clerical banalities, as invariable as jokes in Punch; *sometimes, in deference to the 20th century, lacing the sad brew with references to the United Nations,* apartheid *and the birth pill. He doubtless feels himself to be redundant. The villagers stoically die without his ministrations; they would resent any interruption of their evening telly if he ventured to make a call, and have for long accustomed themselves to cope without benefit of clergy with minor misfortunes like pregnancy and delinquency. In the large cities the situation is not dissimilar.*[3]

Is It Different In America?

There are many who would say, "That's Great Britain. It's different in America." And it is true that many of the statistics bear out such a contention. Gallup polls conducted near the end of the decade of the 1980s suggested that as many as 94 percent of Americans believe in God, 90 percent pray, more than 80 percent are "sometimes very conscious of God's presence," 70 percent believe that Jesus was God, 65 percent belong to a church or synagogue, and 42 percent attend somewhat regularly.[4] There was a religious tone to much of the political rhetoric in the Reagan years, Christian bookstores appear to be prospering all over the country, and the phenomenon of the "megachurch" has asserted itself in metropolitan areas, indicating a definite trend for the rest of the decade.

But the overall picture from the Gallup polls is not a positive one. While there was a growth pattern among such conservative groups as the Church of the Nazarene, Seventh-Day Adventists, Assemblies of God, Mormons, and Southern Baptists, there was considerable decline in the mainline churches, the so-called "Seven Sisters": Episcopalians, Presbyterians (U.S.A.), United Methodists, Congregationalists, Disciples of Christ, American Baptists, and Lutherans (L.C.A.).[5] Wade Clark Roof and William McKinney, in *American Mainline Religion,* cite figures indicating that between 1952 and 1985 the number of people in the U.S. showing a preference for one of the mainline denominations dropped 15 percent.[6] Other statistics reveal that between 1967 and 1984, a period of only 17 years, the Christian Church/Disciples of Christ declined in membership by 40 percent, the Presbyterian Church, U.S.A., by 27 percent, the Episcopalians by 19 percent, the United Church of Christ by 17 percent, and the United Methodist Church by 16 percent.[7] Commenting on similar statistics, William H. Willimon and Robert L. Wilson say: "It is difficult to conceptualize the extent of such a decline. Every week for a decade and a half these denominations had a net loss of *more than five thousand persons per week*. This is equivalent to closing one local church of almost seven hundred members every day for fifteen years."[8] The operative word in most descriptions of what is happening to the mainline denominations is "hemorrhaging."

Even more demoralizing than the losses indicated in these figures is the fact that the largest proportion of the losses is among young adults, who are normally the church leaders of the next generation. According to Gallup and Castelli, 21 percent of Episcopalians and Presbyterians were under 30 in 1983, and only 17 percent in 1987; 32 percent of Disciples of Christ were under 30 in 1983, and only 26 percent in 1987.[9]

Bishop Richard B. Wilke of the United Methodist Church suggested in the mid-80s that these raw statistics do not begin to reveal the true weakening of the mainline churches, which is more apparent in the "inner" statistics about church school participation and leadership resources. During the quadrennium 1960-1964, reported the bishop, 4.2 million persons took an active part in United Methodist Sunday schools. Twenty years later, in the quadrennium 1980-1984, this number had declined to 2.1 million, an almost incredible drop of 50 percent! The number of United Methodist teachers and workers declined in the same period from 540,000 to 420,000, with many pastors considering the church schools irrelevant to the overall mission of their churches and most laity believing that "teaching the faith is for someone else to do."[10]

A recent study called "What the Polls Don't Show: A Closer Look at U.S. Church Attendance," conducted by Kirk Hadaway, Penny Marler, and Mark Chaves, confirms Wilke's pessimism. Based partly on actual head counts in numerous churches, this study shows that the Gallup poll figures for church attendance in the U.S. are considerably more optimistic than the reality admits. The Gallup poll for 1992 reported church attendance at 45 percent of Protestants and 51 percent of Catholics. The true figures, say Hadaway, Marler and Chaves, are 20 percent of Protestants and 28 percent of Catholics — in the case of Protestants, less then half the number shown by the Gallup poll!

Yet another indication of mainline deterioration is the precipitate decline in the number of foreign missionaries fielded by the various denominations. William R. Hutchison points out in an article titled "Americans in World Mission: Revision and Realignment" that from 1935 to 1980 the number of career personnel in Protestant foreign missions plummeted from 10,000 to 3,000. During the same period, the total number of American missionaries in foreign countries increased from 11,000 to 35,000.[11] This means that, while the Protestant mission efforts were experiencing a falloff of 70 percent — a dramatic drop in anybody's book! — conservative, fundamentalist, evangelical, and pentecostal groups increased their efforts by an amazing 3,200 percent.

The Triumph Of Conservatism

What has been occurring among these groups in the same time-frame, when mainline Protestantism has been in a downward spiral, is another story. As early as 1972, Dean M. Kelley, a lawyer doing research for the National Council of Churches, showed in *Why Conservative Churches Are Growing* that American churches since the 1950s have been growing in *inverse* proportion to their openness and ecumenicity. The fastest growth has occurred among Jehovah's Witnesses,

Churches of Christ, Latter-Day Saints (Mormons), Seventh-Day Adventists, the Church of God, and Pentecostalists, all highly exclusivist in membership and anti-ecumenical in attitude. Only slightly less faster-growing have been the Southern Baptists, Missouri Synod Lutherans, and Russian and Greek Orthodox churches, still easily among the more conservative churches in the nation. The mainstream churches, which have all grown increasingly inclusivist and have taken an active part in the ecumenical movement of the last 50 years, are the ones that are losing members.[12]

Martin Marty reads part of the mainline decline in terms of a greater freedom of choice for disgruntled conservatives. Half a century ago, he says, mainline churches counted on restless conservatives for a large number of their new members. People who became discontent with the doctrinaire theology, stringent moralism, or social inadequacy of their conservative or fundamentalist churches normally moved up the ladder into the easier, more respectable mainline churches. But several things have happened to staunch this flow from "lower" to "higher." Now it is easier to escape church religion altogether into the realm of private faith or nonfaith. Little respectability is attached to being a member of *any* church. Family and social pressures to conform have diminished. As mainline churches grew more and more diffuse, with hazier and hazier doctrinal identification, they ceased to be "magnets of loyalty." And, perhaps most important of all, evangelicalism, as it moved into more visibility and respectability, offered a much greater variety of opportunities for movers than it did 50 years ago.[13]

We should not overdraw the growth of the conservative and evangelical churches, however, for in terms of overall numbers their success is relatively small. The number of unchurched Americans has grown at a much faster pace than the number of new members in these churches, and there is evidence that some of these churches are now slowing in their rate of acquisition. A recent report on Southern Baptist churches suggests that only 30 percent of them are presently in a growth pattern, while 52 percent have plateaued and 18 percent are declining in membership. Younger, more suburban churches account for the primary growth in the denomination, while most inner-city, old neighborhood, and rural churches are failing. Even the churches that are holding their own or growing are doing so, according to the experts, primarily by infusions of members from the declining churches, a process that has been called "the circulation of the saints."[14]

Sagging Power And Visibility

Along with their declining membership, the mainline churches have suffered an enormous loss of power and esteem in the public arena. The general shape of American life and culture were from the beginning profoundly affected by the churches. In the time of the colonies, the Congregationalists, Presbyterians, and Episcopalians fairly controlled the civil and cultural existence of the people. In the nineteenth century, as the country expanded, the Baptists and Methodists followed the frontier westward, building churches and schools and helping to dictate the moral and spiritual tone of the nation. The minister was easily one of the most important figures in the community. Churches were considered among the earliest necessities in a developing region, and people felt better and rested easier when they lived within commuting distance of preaching and the sacraments.

It was this centrality in the life and work of the nation that led Martin E. Marty to speak of "the public church," a church that has as much to do with "ordering faith" as with "saving faith," that is, with constituting the civil, social, and political life of the nation from a theological point of view.[15] It would be impossible to write a history of the American people without dwelling at length on the influence of the various mainline denominations. When the ministers and leaders of these denominations spoke, communities, and even the nation, listened.

William R. Hutchison, the Harvard historian, cites as examples of this symbiotic relationship between church and nation the extremely close ties between the Fosdick brothers, Harry Emerson and Raymond, and the Rockefeller family; the great liberal churchman John R. Mott's friendship with no fewer than nine U.S. presidents; and Reinhold Niebuhr's almost oracular consultative status with leaders of both the academic and foreign policy establishment.[16] He also cites C. Luther Fry's 1931 survey of *Who's Who* biographies, revealing that, of the total 16,600 entries, Episcopalians and Presbyterians accounted for 7,000, Congregationalists for 2,000, and Baptists for 1,500, or, among them, two-thirds of all our national celebrities.[17]

The deliberations of the major church assemblies passed almost imperceptibly into the laws and teachings of the entire country. They established the schools, determined the curricula, educated the leaders, wrote the score, and sounded the pitch of our public life for most of two centuries.

It is obvious to the most casual observer that the mainline churches no longer enjoy this place of power and privilege in the national life. Their assemblies continue to debate public issues and pass resolutions about them, but these resolutions seldom find their way into any kind of national consensus. The increasing pluralism of interests in our country, together with the development of a paralyzing gap between the leadership and the laity of the denominations, has destroyed the univocalism with which the denominations once spoke and has vastly weakened their influence in the public arena.

The conservative, fundamentalist, and evangelical churches have found a far greater unity across denominational lines in recent years and have often been more effective than mainline churches in making their voices heard. During the Reagan years, it was Jerry Falwell, head of the Moral Majority, who assumed the mantle of moral leadership in America. I have personally heard Falwell brag that he could enter the Oval Office at the White House almost anytime he wished, merely by making a phone call and asking for an invitation. Reagan sent him to

Oxford University's English Speaking Union to represent the White House in a debate with the prime minister of New Zealand over the deployment of nuclear arms in nonaggressive nations. When I asked him what he knew about the subject, he jauntily retorted, "Not much, but they'll send someone to brief me on the plane."

When we try to recall instances of the church's appearing in the news over the last several years, we remember Falwell and the Moral Majority, Oral Roberts' death threat from God, Jim Bakker's fall over the Jessica Hahn affair, Jimmy Swaggart's successive sexual scandals, the schism in the Missouri Synod Lutheran Church, the battle for control of the Southern Baptist Convention by militant inerrantists, the announcement that the committee for a new United Methodist hymnal planned to leave out the venerable "Onward, Christian Soldiers" as too militaristic and sexually biased, and the occasional hospitalizations of Billy Graham, now regarded as the elder statesman of evangelicalism and a kind of national institution from being so often photographed with American presidents and published in *Reader's Digest.*

The diversionist publicity in this kind of press attention belied the quiet decay and disruption occurring in the mainstream churches. In the first half of the century, it was the Harry Emerson Fosdicks, Lloyd Douglases, Reinhold Niebuhrs, Douglas Hortons, Henry Pitt Van Dusens, and Paul Tillichs who made headlines in *The New York Times, The Boston Globe,* and *The Los Angeles Times.* But by 1989, Martin Marty could title his review of William R. Hutchison's *Between the Times: The Travail of the Protestant Establishment in America, 1900-1960,* published by Cambridge University Press at the libraries-only price of $39.50, "The Establishment That Was," and could declare that "all the news [about religion] since 1960, or at least 1970, has come from the conservative Protestant flank,"[18] meaning individuals and groups peripheral to mainline Christianity. In 1960, said Marty, the newsmakers and celebrities were, with the exception of Billy Graham, from the establishment ranks of Protestantism, the mainline; today *People* magazine could feature on its cover 10 or 20 conservative leaders without bothering to put their names under the pictures (Marty's definition of true celebrity), yet not a single picture from the establishment churches.

What Has Happened To The Mainline?

Historians and sociologists of religion have suggested several reasons for the decline of the mainstream churches, most of which are plausible and probably contributory.

Leonard I. Sweet attributes at least part of the causality to changes in communication methodology. While a few of the great mainline preachers, such as Harry Emerson Fosdick, Norman Vincent Peale, Ralph Sockman, and Robert Schuller pioneered in the use of radio, television, publications, and computerized mailings to reach the masses, by far the largest group of Protestant clergy were content "to remain inky-fingered, acting as if the communications revolution had never taken place." The failure to move into mass media with power and imagination led to a basic failure of rhetoric — "the inability to use the symbolic language that can effectively mobilize church members in an electronic culture."[19]

Robert Wuthnow, the Princeton sociologist, says in *The Struggle for America's Soul* that the two major social movements of the '60s, the civil rights movement and the antiwar movement, publicly revealed the fundamental hypocrisy of the mainline churches and the culture they had helped to form. Then, while liberal voices insisted that we stop talking so much about our value system and begin to enact it, the conservatives accused the liberals of being "thin" on God, moved in to trumpet the old values, and won over large segments of the American populace.[20]

There is much to be said for this argument. Sidney Mead, often called "the Dean of American Church Historians," has long contended that America, in the words of G.K. Chesterton, is "a nation with the soul of a church."[21] That is,

26

America, with its democratic ideal, is an umbrella for sheltering the various religious faiths of Americans and for carrying out the will of God. During the 1960s and 1970s, liberal Christians lost their faith in the country and its idealism, and effectively broke off from the center. Conservative Christians made the most of this divorce, wrapping themselves in the flag and identifying themselves as the prototypical Christian Americans.

The mainline churches can of course hardly be called liberal, for most of their adherents are at least traditional, if not conservative, in both religion and politics. But the effect of the period has been a general weakening of the mainline reputation, and, with that, a growing uncertainty among mainline members about their ecclesiastical identity and purpose. Some of them have abandoned their former churches to join the more clearly defined conservative and fundamentalist churches. Others have taken sides within their local congregations and refought on a small scale the battle over theology and style that has been going on in American Christianity as a whole for the past 75 years.[22] And undoubtedly many others have learned to live without church altogether.

The default of the mainstream churches has left our society without the moral and theological guidance it enjoyed for the first two centuries of its existence — a condition Richard J. Neuhaus called "the naked public square"[23] — and now it must be doubly confusing to old mainstreamers, whose voices are no longer welcome, to see the aggressiveness of such conservatives and fundamentalists as Pat Robertson, Jerry Falwell, and Charles Stanley, who are doing their best to fill the vacuum and influence culture the way the great liberal leaders once did.

"For a long time 'outsiders' to the mainline, religious conservatives now hope for a stronger hold on the culture," say Roof and McKinney. "They have successfully called up the old symbols of American civil religion and forged a new alliance between belief in God and belief in America. If religious liberals are pessimistic and alienated from democratic faith, conservatives are optimistic and are ready to proclaim anew

27

that what is good for the country is good for the gospel and vice versa — a message Americans have often enjoyed hearing, and one that resonated extremely well in the seventies and eighties.''[24]

"The Troeltschian Solution"

Robert Bellah, in the widely read book *Habits of the Heart: Individualism and Commitment in American Life,* considers helpful an explanation of what is occurring in Ernst Troeltsch's division of the Christian spectrum into "church," "sect," and "mysticism" or "religious individualism." The church enters the world culturally and socially, seeking to change it, while the sect stands apart from the world, regarding it as sinful. Mysticism or religious individualism focuses primarily on individuals and the disciplines whereby they can know God privately, regardless of their way of relating to the world.

From the time of the Puritans until recently, the church type was predominant in America, with strong interaction between religious leaders and government. There have always been sectarian movements, of course, such as the German pietists, the Mormons, and the Pentecostalists, and there have been notable mystical figures such as Ralph Waldo Emerson, Rufus Jones, and Elton Trueblood. But by and large it was the church view that held sway, with strong and beneficent reciprocal relations between the mainline denominations and the general culture.

Bellah speaks appreciatively of the role of the mainline churches:

> *They have offered a conception of God as neither wholly other nor a higher self, but rather as involved in time and history. These churches have tried to develop a larger picture of what it might mean to live a biblical life in America. They have sought to be communities of*

memory, to keep in touch with biblical sources and histor-ical traditions not with literalist obedience but through an intelligent reappropriation illuminated by historical and theological reflection. They have tried to relate bib-lical faith and patience to the whole of contemporary life — cultural, social, political, economic — not just to per-sonal and family morality. They have tried to steer a mid-dle course between mystical fusion with the world and sectarian withdrawal from it.[25]

Throughout the first two centuries of American life, says Bellah, the religious intellectuals in the mainline churches spoke for the society as a whole. But now, during the last genera-tion, this has not been true. Those same intellectuals have be-come more and more remote from the cultural center. Failing to produce another Tillich or a Niebuhr who could become the focus of fruitful controversy and discussion, they have retreated into specialization, blandness, and faddism, leaving the high ground to the conservatives and fundamentalists, who have rallied successfully, formed new churches, networked with other sectarians, promoted conservatism in politics, secured the endorsement of presidents, established new publishing houses, colleges, and seminaries, taken over cable religious programming, put their heroes in the public eye, and ostensi-bly called the nation back to the values that made it great in the past.

The sectarians have waved the flag, glorified militarism and jingoism, come down hard on homosexuality and abortion, bolstered male chauvinism and big-time sports, insisted on bib-lical literalism as the bedrock of all theological understand-ing, and ridiculed all other forms of religion as godless, demonic, anti-Christian hogwash. For the folks who have preferred certainty to subtlety and trumpets to oboes, they have provided these, and their burgeoning, clamorous following, among those who don't know better, probably looks more like the church than the church itself.

The mystics and religious individualists, in the meantime, have been enjoying their own field day, with such fads, trends,

29

and serious enterprises as Zen, channeling, crystal consciousness, pyramid power, witchcraft, ecology, goddess worship, shamanism, communes, harmonic convergence, Tarot reading, reincarnation, and extraterrestrial communication. They have even developed alternative forms of prayer, liturgy, and sacred writings, and their hymns can be heard in the synthetic wave music being played in any esoteric tearoom or bookstore in America. Together, they comprise what is known as the New Age religion, a compendium of individualism and self-consciousness teachings from such diverse sources as Buddhism, Hinduism, Christianity, Gnosticism, Zoroastrianism, Tao, I Ching, Ralph Waldo Emerson, Henry David Thoreau, C.G. Jung, Edgar Cayce, Fritz Perls, L. Ron Hubbard, and Shirley MacLaine.

Russell Chandler, religion writer for *The Los Angeles Times,* says that the bottom line for all New Age thought can be stated in three words: "All is One." The cosmos is pure, undifferentiated energy, a consciousness or life force, and everything is a single great, interconnected process. "There is nothing that *isn't* God. Human beings are a mode, or an expression of, the God who is a principle, a consciousness, a life force."[26]

Jesus, for New Agers, is usually considered one of the great masters of humanity, but not exclusively a savior. He had the higher consciousness, but so did Buddha, Mahomet, Confucius, Lao-Tse, St. Francis, St. Teresa, Gandhi, and numerous other luminaries in human history. The important thing, in New Age doctrine, is not to attach oneself to great religious figures but to discover the same relationship within oneself to the all-encompassing spirit that has flowed through them. Thus the emphasis is both mystical and individualistic, ideally fulfilling Troeltsch's definition of the third form of religious communion.

With a few exceptions, such as the recent brouhaha over the "Re-Imagining" Conference, mainline Christianity characteristically accepts New Age religion with a grain of salt, seeing it as a sometimes helpful, sometimes kooky exfoliation

of America's religious idealism, much of which was originally inspired by the church and its more orthodox teachings. After all, transcendentalism, New Age's direct forebear in the
nineteenth century, was a product of the fusing of Oriental
thought with the official teachings of New England divinity
schools. While the truth of any New Age philosophy must always be judged against the plumb line of biblical revelation,
the whole phenomenon is a relatively harmless excrescence of
vital religion and, with reference to its emphasis on love, ecology, holistic foods, simple lifestyle, reverence for life, and
respect for cultural differences, a positive force in the radial
culture.

Not so, of course, for the sectarians, who view the New
Age as the work of the devil and a sign that the end of all things
must be close at hand. They faithfully scour the literature of
fellow Christians for any references to the seductive, hellish
writings or doctrines of New Age practitioners, and preach ex-
coriating sermons against such convenient bogeymen as gnosticism, reincarnation, channeling, and witchcraft. With their gift
for religious paranoia, they delight in exploiting the fear and
bewilderment of their constituents by warning of this glittering array of heretical ways and notions surrounding them on
the cultural horizon.

The New Middle Class

Sociologist Peter Berger, writing in the "How My Mind
Has Changed" series in *The Christian Century*, offers yet
another hypothesis to explain the failure of mainline religion.
What has happened, he says, is that the middle-class society
and culture that are the natural habitat of the Protestant
churches have undergone a seismic change. In America, as well
as in other advanced capitalistic societies, the middle class has
split, so that, in addition to the old middle class, centered in
the business community and the professions, there is now "a
new middle class, based on the production and distribution

of symbolic knowledge, whose members are the increasingly large number of people occupied with education, the media of mass communication, therapy in all its forms, the advocacy and administration of well-being, social justice and personal lifestyles."[27]

This new middle class, which is on the whole younger and better educated than the old middle class and largely controls the communications network of the society, includes many of the clergy and officials of the mainline churches. By virtue of their education, associations, and reference groups, they managed to become the leaders of these churches. Predictably, the old middle class, instinctively fearful of their new leadership and what it would mean both to their institutions and their personal lives, became resistant. In some cases, they have remained in their churches and fought the leadership for control. But in most cases, says Berger, not wishing to spend their time and energy in institutional conflict, they simply "voted with their pocketbooks and their feet; they reduced their contributions and, in large numbers, they left."[28]

Berger's theory meshes well with the observation of James Davison Hunter that there is a greater disparity between the elite and the laity of the mainline churches than there is in the conservative and evangelical churches. This gap, says Hunter, exists not only in terms of social and educational background but in the level of intellectual discourse as well. While average church members are probably looking for moral formulae, even slogans, for living, the clergy and leaders of the mainline denominations are inclined to give them intellectual circumlocutions and abstractions.[29]

A massive self-study done by scholars and administrators in the Christian Church/Disciples of Christ reaches a similar conclusion. It observes repeatedly that Disciples ministers tend to receive their theological and ministerial formation in liberal institutions such as Yale Divinity School, the Divinity School of the University of Chicago, Bright Divinity School, and Lexington Theological Seminary, then become pastors of churches in a predominantly rural denomination. A poll of the theological orientations of clergy in three denominations, Baptist, Presbyterian, and Disciples, is very revealing. Here is a brief example of the results:[30]

	Percent "Strongly Agree" or "Agree"		
	Baptist	**Presbyterian**	**Disciples**
Jesus as only way to salvation	97	65	46
Devil actually exists	96	49	37
Jesus will return to earth someday	96	56	38
Virgin birth a biological miracle	94	56	42
Hell is a real place	91	38	34
Adam and Eve real historical persons	86	21	20

Even the most casual glance at this chart is sufficient to remind us of Dean Kelley's observation in *Why Conservative Churches Are Growing* that the stricter churches, both theologically and morally, will tend to do better in the ecclesiastical marketplace than the liberal churches. Southern Baptists have continued to grow slightly in recent years, Presbyterians have lost ground, and the record of the Disciples churches has been disastrous.

The Bottom Line

What is the bottom-line result of all this for the socio-religious situation? The sum of it is that both strong, sectarian religion and the aura of semi-religious practices known as New Age have both made obvious gains during the past few decades, while mainline religion, which once held the cultural hegemony in this country, has lost its position of power and influence, as well as many of its adherents. This rise in the fortunes of two of the elements of the Troeltschian formula, sects and mysticism, despite the decline of the third, the mainline church, accounts for the relative stability of American religion in the polls, which continue to indicate that a large majority of our people believe in God and that church-going is almost as popular as ever.

But the pastors of most mainline churches know, as far as their own congregations are concerned, that the figures lie. The median age of their congregations is steadily advancing, it becomes harder and harder to sustain effective youth programs, the cost of managing church plants with sufficient staff members to care for perceived congregational needs is pulling away from the size of offerings and available funds, and fewer and fewer of the people who do attend church appear to have any grasp at all of the great fundamental teachings of the faith or a corresponding sense of commitment to the perpetuation or augmentation of the faith.

The Forest Or The Trees?

It is my personal conclusion that most of the reasons given by the historians and sociologists for shifts and changes in the religious scene, while basically correct in their own ways, generally neglect the more cosmic issues reshaping life in our time. They are primarily the result, in other words, of looking at the trees and not the forest. If we really want to understand what is happening to the mainline church, we have to step back further and look at a broader picture. We must get an overview of what is happening to our entire global culture, for that determines, more than anything else, the configuration of patterns within particular areas of the human enterprise.

Take the sheer force of social pluralism, for example. Travel facilities, communications media, and immigration patterns have conspired in recent years to alter drastically the population makeup of many areas of the world. Vast segments of America are becoming "metropolitanized," with immigrant ethnic groups occupying large sections of what were once predominantly white Anglo-European enclaves. The resulting changes in churches in these areas are enormous. The Roman Catholic Church, for instance, has become more Hispanic than Irish. The Black Muslim movement, that offers pride and status to young black males, has been so successful in New York,

Chicago, Detroit, and other metropolitan areas that there are now more Muslims in those cities than Episcopalians or Presbyterians. And the rights of these Americans, so long neglected, are now being sought at the expense of the rights of those who traditionally enjoyed power and superiority in the national system.

The whole "rights" revolution in our time, that has resulted in the near paralysis of the entire legal system, has also had enormous impact on the religious situation. Mary Ann Glendon, in her fascinating study *Rights Talk*, contends that the high degree of individuation springing from the venerable rights tradition in the American way of life has led us all to be so sensitive about our personal rights that now, in the last 30 years, we are engaged in a great standoff of one person's rights against another's.

"A rapidly expanding catalog of rights — extending to trees, animals, smokers, nonsmokers, consumers, and so on — not only multiplies the occasions for collisions," she says, "but it risks trivializing core democratic values. A tendency to frame nearly every social controversy in terms of a clash of rights (a woman's right to her own body vs. a fetus' right to life) impedes compromise, mutual understanding, and the discovery of common ground. A penchant for absolute formulations ('I have the right to do whatever I want with my property') promotes unrealistic expectations and ignores both social costs and the rights of others."[31]

What Glendon is saying is that we have reached the point in the American consciousness where we are basically unable to subordinate our own rights and interests to the rights and interests of others, or to those of larger entities that once subsumed the individual. In the absoluteness with which we hold to our rights, we live with unrealistic expectations, engage in heightened social conflict, and often forgo the dialogue and flexibility that would lead to consensus or accommodation. In short, we make social engagement more and more difficult.

That this is true in the churches nearly goes without saying. Members are much less likely today to submerge their own interests in the overall interests of the institutions to which they belong. They are far more strident in asserting personal viewpoints, more eager to get what is due them, more combative with those who appear to oppose them or to stand between them and what they desire. They vote not only with their pocketbooks and with their feet, as Berger suggested, but with their tongues, openly complaining to their ministers and broadcasting their unhappiness both inside and outside the walls of the church. One minister I know went to the trouble of attempting to trace the history of six dissidents in his congregation, and found that at least five of them had left a trail of contumacy and broken relationships in various churches in the community. An interview with each of them convinced him that they were not at fault individually, but that "the temper of the times" had resulted in their being unable to settle into a single congregation and find fulfillment there.

Robert Bellah and his colleagues have traversed similar ground in their most recent book, *The Good Society*.[32] The American experiment, they claim, was founded largely on the philosophical notions of John Locke, a Calvinist who taught that private property is the basis for all realistic public morality. But the designers of the American constitution managed to detach the secular aspects of Locke's teachings from his overall vision and create a philosophy of individual rights largely divorced from any sense of subordination to a divine will or redeemed community. With the growth of corporations in the nineteenth century, which were treated before the law as private persons with inviolable rights, we developed both a state and an economy that seemed to exist beyond the control of the citizens, and hence we have come to be innately suspicious of institutions and despondent about our ability to manage them for the benefit of all. As in recent years through constant exposés in the media we have become increasingly aware of the culpability of institutions, we have tended to reject responsibility for them and, in effect, to abandon them to their perversity.

Thus we see a growing disaffection for institutions in general, resulting in frequent outbursts and demonstrations against government at all levels, in increasing litigation against churches, hospitals, mental care organizations, and schools and universities, and in a high level of complaints against the leadership, programming, and ministry of local churches. Where people once accepted the failures of the institutions as reflections of a general malaise or extensions of their own failures as persons and members of the whole, today they increasingly blame the institutions for their own unhappiness and complain that everything in the world is going bad.

Conservative and fundamentalist spokespersons have been quick to respond to this general attitude and to turn it on the mainline churches as if they were responsible for the ills of society. In a *Christianity Today* review of Ari L. Goldman's *The Search for God at Harvard*, for example, the reviewer concludes a sniping resumé of the book, which is about the experiences of a *New York Times* religion writer, an Orthodox Jew, during a year spent at Harvard Divinity School, by taking a healthy swipe at mainline Protestantism, which he apparently holds responsible for the diversity and lack of evangelicalism at the school. "Indeed," writes Doug LeBlanc, "an education in the theological crucible that is Harvard Divinity School should be ideal training for ministry in the wildly eclectic culture of mainline Protestantism. A student who enters and leaves Harvard Divinity as an evangelical will be able to withstand almost anything else from mainline Protestantism."[33]

Alvin Toffler, the noted synthesizer of cultural trends who coined the phrase *Future Shock*, speaks even more sweepingly of the psychological and political changes taking place in our time. He caps a quarter-century of global studies with the observation that the modern world is undergoing a massive transformation in the way it regards and relates to basic, elemental power. "We live at a moment when the entire structure of power that held the world together is now disintegrating," says Toffler. "A radically different structure of power is taking form. And this is happening at every level of human society."[34]

The old patterns of power and organization are fracturing in every direction, he says. National and international structures are toppling, cities are becoming increasingly unworkable, businesses are losing their old hierarchical shape, political authority is no longer what it once was, workers, students, and family members don't accept arrangements under which they once lived, racial and gender subordination is being overthrown, people don't even accept the theological rationales that once satisfied them. Everything in the world is being redefined. A revolutionary new system is coming into place.

Historically, according to Toffler, there have been three bases of power: violence, wealth, and knowledge. Whoever controlled the power base in any given era ruled the world. In the earlier periods of history, it was the rulers and feudal landlords who held control because they had the muscle to enforce their will. Then, with the coming of the age of trading, exploration, and manufacturing, the power base shifted to a larger class of people, those who possessed wealth. Even kings and emperors began to depend on bankers and tycoons for their power. Finally, in our own time, the essence of power is beginning to be located not with the rulers or even with the bankers but with the managers of knowledge. The computer has ushered us into an age in which power is more diffused than ever, when whiz kids with laptop machines can manipulate the symbolic language of a new economy to create new empires or bring down old ones overnight. Wealth, status, position, land, connections, all the old formulas for success, are falling before the power of the new knowledge to reorganize corporations, remanage politics, reinvent products, and redesign human existence. And, while the old forms of power were always limited, this new one is virtually limitless, for it is infinitely expandable and nonexclusive.

There is no point in trying to oppose this transformation. It is one of those cultural tidal waves (Toffler's second book was called *The Third Wave)* that occur periodically in the history of the world and that are unstoppable, that simply sweep everything before them. The sooner we realize this, the sooner we can cease expending our energy on the futile attempt to hold everything where it was and begin to invest it in reshaping the future.

Consider this schematization of the three great ages of humanity as we are now able to view them:

The Three Ages Of Humanity

	Agrarian	Industrial	Computer
Important to Success	Land, force	Wealth	Knowledge
Knowledge	Preliterate; folk knowledge	Literate; scientific development	Postliterate; images & symbols
Government	Feudal	Movement toward democracy	Global democracy; networking
Sense of Time	Natural; sun and seasons	Use of clocks; scheduling	Constant (e.g., laptops)
Employment of Force	Physical; brute labor	Mechanized; machines doing much of labor	Technicized; machines managing machines
Religion	Sacramental, close to life; dependent on birth	More intellectual; growth of denominations	Highly individual and ecumenical
Goal of Life	Survive, reproduce	Attain "The Good Life" here and hereafter	Self-realization & self-fulfillment

Sketchy as it is, a diagram like this permits us to understand some things that are otherwise difficult to comprehend. Under the rubric "Knowledge," for example, the fact that we are entering a postliterate age in which electronic images and symbols are more important than books (something Marshall McLuhan tried to tell us years ago in *Understanding Media*) helps to explain why our educational methods are failing today and nearly a fourth of the adult U.S. population is functionally illiterate. Most education is still geared to the old literate system, while most children are raised in postliterate homes, watching television, playing computer games, and looking at magazines that are really television images pasted up into the semblance of magazines. At some point, we will achieve an educational system completely geared to the new era and abandon our frustration about trying to retain the system with which those of us in an older generation grew up.

By the same token, our Bible derives from the Agrarian age that was preliterate and characterized by folk knowledge — by stories, proverbs, and mnemonic sayings. The discovery of movable print and growth of literacy at the end of the Middle Ages and beginning of the modern period led to a rediscovery of the Bible as a printed phenomenon, and a whole religious culture grew up around the Word and commentaries on the Word. But the growth of science in the Industrial period also challenged the absolute veracity of the folk knowledge from the Agrarian era and issued in the battle over the Bible that has torn much of Christendom in our time. Now we are in the Computer age, when many people can relate to the Bible again as a book of folk stories and images (preliterate) better than as a book of theology or doctrine, and take a much more selective, electronic approach to it than their forebears in the Industrial age.

In terms of "Government," we note that the Industrial age, when the value of land gave way to naked wealth, carried the peoples of the world inevitably toward more and more democratic forms of policy, and the advent of the Computer age, with instant communication around the world and the globalization of business (the pattern is for large corporations not to have a "home" office any more in the country of origin, but to have a number of bases throughout the world, linked by sophisticated communications systems), leads us increasingly into complete global democracy. In recent examples of totalitarian suppression, say, the revolt in China and the attempted coup in the old Soviet Union, news of the actions was immediately broadcast to the entire world via telephones, fax machines, and even satellite television. Eventually, old-style dominance by brutalization will become impossible in a world where informed social pressures conspire to prevent it.

Looking at "Religion," we see that the style in the Agrarian age was very elemental and sacramental, usually with direct correspondence between the worshiper and the result of the worship (for example, a farmer worshiped the deity of fertility and expected a favorable crop yield), and that most people had the religion they inherited by circumstances of birth (Hindus begat Hindus; Catholics, Catholics; Muslims, Muslims). Following the Reformation, and increasingly during the Industrial period, which we remember was a time of focus on literacy, many people elected to belong to religious groups outside the ones in which they were born. In Christendom, there developed extraordinary passions about the particular groups or denominations that were chosen, and the religion spread rapidly everywhere by fissiparous action, with groups constantly breaking off to form new groups. As we move more and more into the Computer age, however, we begin to discern a diminishing of this pattern as people become more highly individuated and care less about the external particularities that once spawned denominations. Their goal now is more private, to discover the true inner nature of the self and to find individual ways of expressing the self.

Many contemporary phenomena can be more readily understood under the terms of such a diagram. The great debate over abortion is really a clash between those on one hand who sense the transformation of human existence from an age of extensive social control to an age of privatization and

41

individual choice and those on the other who are trying to restrain the transformation. The universal drug problem is related to the widespread social malaise that always accompanies an epochal shift, when ideologies appear to fail and the future is uncertain, and is complicated by the fact that the movement toward individualism and privatization has occurred faster than our ability to educate people about the responsibility and self-control needed for life in the new era. The many liberation movements of the last quarter-century — racial, sexual, gender, age — are directly related to entering a new era in which the stereotypes of the former age are no longer applicable (think how the dawn of the Industrial period invalidated old conceptions of serfdom and social immobility). The American economic malaise may be at least partially attributed to the globalization of business and American industry's pride and insularity at a time when Germany, Japan, and other nations disabled by war and having to play catch-up have shown great imagination and aggressiveness in entering the new era. It is little wonder, in a time of such upheaval, that theologians are not writing *summas* as Barth and Tillich did a few years ago, and that theology today, as poet Chad Walsh said in *God at Large* resembles "a drunken man, staggering from one side of the road to the other."[35] As Robert McAfee Brown says in *Theology in a New Key,* the *summas* have been replaced by *ad hoc* conferences, xeroxed papers, and the products of fax machines.

It does not matter whether the formulaic expressions describing life in each of the three major eras of humanity are totally accurate in their details. The important thing is to begin to perceive from such a diagram how completely human existence is altered and transformed in passing from one age to the next. Looking back, we can see the dramatic and irreversible effects of moving out of the agrarian period into the industrial period. All human life within the boundaries of civilization (and sometimes outside the boundaries as well) was profoundly changed by entering a new era. Sensibilities were altered, populations were rearranged, thought was transformed political life was restructured, literally *everything* became different. Now we must not be blind to the fact that another epochal upheaval is occurring and that we are swiftly moving into a similar era of renewal and transformation. The signs are undeniable. More than many are willing to admit, the process is almost a *fait accompli*. We are waking up in a new world.

Granted that this is true, what does it mean for religion in our time? At the very least, it portends a breaking up of former religious structures and new ways of relating to religious understanding. Just as the massive shifting of cultural underpinnings at the end of the Middle Ages (with the breakdown of feudalism, the discovery of movable type, the advent of the monetary system, the exploration of the world and concomitant growth of trade, and the general impetus to new thought) resulted in the Protestant Reformation and the beginnings of denominationalism, the incredible movement occurring in the last half-century is already in the process of casting down old forms and raising up new ones. We are in an era not only of "powershift" but of "mindshift," when ways of viewing life on this planet are being profoundly altered.

Loren Mead has described our transitional era in *The Once and Future Church* as a time of shifting paradigms. In the early years of the church, he says, Christians lived in the Apostolic Paradigm, when the church's existence was defined in terms of its mission to a hostile environment. Then, with the establishment under Constantine of Christianity as the religion of the empire, we entered the Christendom Paradigm, when the immediate environment was no longer hostile and mission was redefined as pertaining to pagan nations on the edge of the empire. This model or paradigm persisted even through the Reformation, with the various denominations still perceiving their *raison d'etre* as the conversion of unbelievers in distant places. We are presently in a time between paradigms, says Mead, when many congregations are attempting to hold on to the old paradigm yet it clearly isn't functioning as it did. But one thing is clear in the new, highly secularized age we have entered: the church's mission lies once more at its front door; we no longer exist in a Christian environment.[36]

The conservatives and fundamentalists are reacting to the changes in an expected way: they are opposed to them. They appear temporarily to be triumphing over the mainline churches because they are able to capitalize on people's natural fears and hesitancies about entering a forcefield of change and renewal. They champion the doctrines, moral standards, and accountable structures of an earlier period and promise to return life to its former peace and stability. But they will inevitably lose the battle, for they are contending not only with human religious and political forces but with the inexorable turning of a culture. Only those who recognize what is transpiring and align themselves with the movement in such a way as to regain some power to shape the new era may be said to "win" in any final or definitive sense.

This does not mean that there will be no continuity between the past and the future. On the contrary, there is always continuity from one era to another, especially in the areas of personal spirituality and love for others, which lay at the heart of Jesus' teachings in his own time of great disturbance. But the structures of organizations, the overall way in which power and authority are shaped and exercised, are always toppled like the stones of the temple in Jerusalem.

All of this is to say that the minor failures of the mainline denominations — their awkwardness with the media, the hypocrisy that showed up in the crises of the '60s, the erosion of their consensus, their lack of dynamic new leadership, the widening gap between clergy and laity, their failure to take politically correct stands on large popular issues of the day, their inability to deal with pluralism — are just that, minor failures. They have had worse problems at other moments in their history and survived them. Their time is simply up. Hurled into existence by the cataclysms of history and culture, they are now dying, as other institutions are dying. All the efforts to renew them, to reinvent them, to pump new life into them, will fail.

It does not mean that God is dead or that Christianity is at an end or that the church will cease to exist. On the contrary, all three have been perceived as being most alive in the very passages of time when great cultural shifts were occurring and humanity was passing through one of its occasional "dark nights of the soul." We may have to "reinvent the church," as Loren Mead says; but the results of such a reinvention may be far less negative than we now fear.

An Explanation For What Is Happening

What this massive cultural transformation *does* explain is the disarray that is occurring on the church scene today and the distress that has resulted in the life of the average congregation and its members. Everybody is under bombardment. The structures are slipping and disintegrating around all our parishioners. The world economy is changing, their jobs are at risk, their children don't obey or respect them, their marriages and family lives are shaky, their sense of well-being is at an all-time low, their self-esteem is almost nonexistent, their faith doesn't seem to provide any answers, and their church is failing them. It is no wonder they are angry with their ministers and leaders, or that they shift from congregation to congregation, searching for answers they are not likely to find in any of them.

Richard Neuhaus may say that it is only a "public and scholarly illusion that American society has been secularized"[37] because the polls show that so many people say they still believe in God and Christ and the devil. But the truth is that people are far more subtly and profoundly secularized than we have realized. For years they have been progressively undergoing what Andrew Delbanco in *The Puritan Ordeal* calls the process of "disenchantment," of coming to believe that the things that happen to them and the world around them are not the will of God or the will of the devil but merely happen, gratuitously and without cosmic plan or permission.[38] They no longer see

America as God's new Israel, as the redemptive nation established in a new Garden of Eden, and they do not believe that God will now miraculously rescue us from the confusion, crime, and corruption that grip our leadership and institutions. They feel increasingly abandoned to fate, like inhabitants of a planet gone awry or a spaceship that has lost touch with its control unit. It is possibly only a matter of time until Americans will openly desert their churches as the British have already deserted theirs and we will look sadly upon the twin symbols of our culture, the sleek silos of nuclear power stations and the broken battlements of the churches, with a sense of profound yearning and nostalgia.

Perhaps the most hopeful note on which to end this chapter is the one with which John Wilson of Princeton concludes the several essays in *Altered Landscapes*. After noting the enormity of the changes occurring in religion in America, Wilson comments on the significant continuity that is there as well. Americans, he observes, have always expected and generated transformation in their dealings with the continent they inhabit. The very sweep of our culture from East to West has built a sense of creative change into our psyches. Theologically, says Wilson, Americans have therefore been much more open to the doctrine of the Holy Spirit than Europeans, for the Spirit stands symbolically for the importance of change in relationship to structure. From the days of the Great Awakening onward, our culture has been explainable in terms of Spirit, movement, and repositioning. "As in no other society, the Holy Spirit, or its cultural equivalent, has become the animating principle of American corporate activity. The cultural outcome is that change (movement) is accorded primacy over form (order) as the foundation of life in this world."[39]

If this theory is correct, the game is by no means over. We are merely trying to readjust to some new rules.

---

1. P.D. James, *Devices and Desires* (New York: Alfred A. Knopf, 1990), p. 89.

2. David Watson, *I Believe in the Church* (Grand Rapids: William B. Eerdmans Publishing Co., 1978), p. 13.

3. Watson, *op.cit.,* pp. 15-16.

4. George Gallup, Jr., and Jim Castelli, *The People's Religion: American Faith in the 90's* (New York: Macmillan Publishing Co., 1989).

5. Gallup and Castelli, *op.cit.,* p. 17.

6. Wade Clark Roof and William McKinney, *American Mainline Religion: Its Changing Shape and Future* (New Brunswick: Rutgers University Press, 1987), p. 16.

7. Cited by Leonard I. Sweet, "The Modernization of Protestant Religion in America," in David W. Lotz et al, eds., *Altered Landscapes: Christianity in America, 1935-1985* (Grand Rapids: William B. Eerdmans Publishing Co., 1989), p. 38.

8. William H. Willimon and Robert L. Wilson, "The Present Crisis: The Impact of the Membership Decline on Mainline Churches," *Quarterly Review,* Fall, 1987, pp. 74-75.

9. Gallup and Castelli, *op.cit.,* p. 27. Roof and McKinney showed in an earlier book, *Liberal Protestantism: Realities and Possibilities,* that this "graying" trend was more pronounced among the mainline churches than among conservative groups. In 1986, 30.2 percent of "moderate" Protestants were over 55 years of age, while only 15.7 percent of "conservative" Protestants were; and, at the same time, the birth average among "liberal" Protestants was 1.97 per woman, among "moderate" Protestants 2.27 per woman, and among "conservative" Protestants 2.54 per woman. (Robert S. Michaelsen and Wade Clark Roof, eds., *Liberal Protestantism: Realities and Possibilities* [New York: Pilgrim Press, 1986], pp. 43-44.) Conservative Christians were not only younger, overall, they were having more babies.

10. Richard B. Wilke, *And Are We Yet Alive?: The Future of the United Methodist Church* (Nashville: Abingdon Press, 1988), pp. 13-15.

11. In David W. Lotz et al, eds., *Altered Landscapes,* p. 155.

12. Dean M. Kelley, *Why Conservative Churches Are Growing* (New York: Harper and Row, 1972), pp. 88-90.

13. Martin E. Marty, *The Public Church: Mainline-Evangelical-Catholic* (New York: Crossroad Publishing Co., 1981), p. 85.

14. Cf. Mark Wingfield, "70 Percent of SBC Churches Are Plateaued or Declining," *The Alabama Baptist*, December 6, 1990, p. 1.

15. Martin E. Marty, *The Public Church,* pp. 16-17.

16. William R. Hutchison, ed., *Between the Times: The Travail of the Protestant Establishment in America, 1900-1960* (Cambridge: Cambridge University Press, 1989), p. 7.

17. Hutchison, *op.cit.,* pp. 11-12.

18. Martin E. Marty, "The Establishment That Was," *The Christian Century,* November 15, 1989, pp. 1045-1047.

19. Sweet, *op.cit.,* p. 28.

20. Robert Wuthnow, *The Struggle for America's Soul: Evangelicals, Liberals, and Secularism* (Grand Rapids: William B. Eerdmans Publishing Co., 1989), pp. 33-34.

21. Sidney E. Mead, *The Nation with the Soul of a Church* (Macon, Georgia: Mercer University Press, 1985).

22. For an excellent description of this controversy, see Bradley J. Longfield, *The Presbyterian Controversy: Fundamentalists, Modernists, and Moderates* (New York: Oxford University Press, 1991). R. Stephen Warner's article on the Presbyterian Church of Mendocino, California, "Mirror for American Protestantism: Mendocino Presbyterian Church in the Sixties and Seventies," in Milton J. Coalter, John M. Mulder, and Louis B. Weeks, *The Mainstream Protestant "Decline": The Presbyterian Pattern* (Louisville: Westminster/John Knox Press, 1990), pp. 198-223, is a vivid description of the struggle of traditionalists and evangelicals within a single congregation.

23. Richard J. Neuhaus, *The Naked Public Square: Religion and Democracy in America* (Grand Rapids: William B. Eerdmans Publishing Co., 1984).

24. Roof and McKinney, *op.cit.,* p. 93.

25. Robert Bellah et al., *Habits of the Heart: Individualism and Commitment in American Life* (San Francisco: Harper and Row, 1985), p. 237.

26. Russell Chandler, *Understanding the New Age* (Dallas: Word Publishing Co., 1988), p. 29.

27. Peter Berger, "Reflections of an Ecclesiastical Expatriate," *The Christian Century,* October 24, 1990, p. 966.

28. Berger, *op.cit.,* p. 967.

29. James Davison Hunter, "American Protestantism: Sorting Out the Present, Looking Toward the Future," in Richard J. Neuhaus, ed., *The Believable Futures of American Protestantism* (Grand Rapids: William B. Eerdmans Publishing Co., 1988), p. 37.

30. D. Newell Williams, ed., *A Case Study of Mainstream Protestantism: The Disciples' Relation to American Culture, 1880-1989* (Grand Rapids: William B. Eerdmans Publishing Co., 1991), p. 367.

31. Mary Ann Glendon, *Rights Talk* (New York: The Free Press, 1991), p. xi.

32. Robert Bellah et al, *The Good Society* (New York: Alfred A. Knopf, 1991).

33. Doug LeBlanc, "Worship at the Relativist Shrine," *Christianity Today,* November 25, 1991, pp. 35-36.

34. Alvin Toffler, *Powershift: Knowledge, Wealth, and Violence at the Edge of the 21st Century* (New York: Bantam Books, 1990), p. 3.

35. Chad Walsh, *God at Large* (New York: Seabury Press, 1971), p. 11.

36. Loren Mead, *The Once and Future Church* (Washington, D.C.: The Alban Institute, 1991).

37. Neuhaus, *The Believable Futures of American Protestantism,* p. 2.

38. Andrew Delbanco, *The Puritan Ordeal* (Cambridge: Harvard University Press, 1989).

39. John F. Wilson, "Religion at the Core of American Culture," in David W. Lotz et al, eds., *Altered Landscapes,* p. 373.

Chapter 2

The Sensibilities Of The Saints

In 1988, friends and former students of Langdon Gilkey produced a *Festschrift* in his honor. It was called *The Whirlwind in Culture: Frontiers in Theology*. The name symbolized our cultural experience of the last 50 years. Gilkey's own autobiographical introduction to the volume "confessed" the windings and turnings in his thought through one of the most tempestuous periods in history.

Raised in the household of a famous minister in Chicago, Charles W. Gilkey, Langdon went off to Harvard, fell under the spell of George Santayana, and became a naturalist and an unbeliever. Then, at the eve of World War II, he heard Reinhold Niebuhr speak about the necessity of holding in tension this corrupt, stricken world with the absolute transcendence of God, and promptly became a Niebuhrian.

When he went off to China to teach English, he was captured by the Japanese and interned for four years in Shantung province with approximately 2,000 other foreigners. There he learned the imperative nature of moral discipline and commitment as the very basis of human survival.

Teaching at Vanderbilt Divinity School in the early sixties, he encountered the black/white conflict in the Old South and resigned in protest against the University's refusal to reinstate James Lawson, a divinity student expelled for leading sit-ins at Nashville lunch counters.

Shortly thereafter, Gilkey's wife left him, taking their adopted son to live in New York. He remarried and accepted a teaching position at the University of Chicago. But he was a different man, humbled and broken by his marital experience, and "newly conscious of how precarious every aspect of good fortune is, how deeply confused and misguided we remain, and how uncertain is every step we take."[1]

Noting the vast changes in the Roman Catholic church after the beginning of Vatican II, Gilkey applied for a fellowship to study the implications of those changes for Protestant theology, and in 1965, after reading intensively in Karl Rahner and Bernard Lonergan, went to Rome for a year as an observer. He met Hans Kung and Edward Schillebeeckx, came in contact with "the fascination and power of the Roman ecclesia," and felt his life and thought spinning through another revolution.

Back in Chicago, he continued to explicate the Death of God movement initiated by his friends Tom Altizer, Bill Hamilton, and Paul Van Buren, and produced two books, *Naming the Whirlwind*[2] and *Religion and the Scientific Future*[3], in which he struggled to make sense of religion in a world that was becoming increasingly secular and agnostic. Because of the latter book, he was invited in 1981 to stand as a witness for the ACLU at the famous "Creationist" trial in Little Rock, Arkansas, and this experience in turn led to his writing *Creationism on Trial: Evolution and God in Little Rock*.[4]

One final turning of his mind, Gilkey recalls, commenced in 1975, when he spent four months as a visiting professor at the University of Kyoto, in Japan, and had an opportunity to witness the way a Buddhist and Shintoist culture adapted itself to a changing technological world order. His wife, meanwhile, had become involved with the Sikh movement in

America, and together they were practicing yoga and spending several weekends each year at a yoga center in New Mexico. All of this inspired a deep interest in non-Christian religions and how Christians can "do theology" in a pluralistic context, affirming both their own stance and those of devotees in other faiths.

Gilkey is admittedly an unusual individual, equipped by background, training, and aptitude for living in the whirlwind. He has survived the changes admirably, in a sense even enjoying a career as an interpreter of the rapidly altering situation. But what of the millions of ordinary people more poorly outfitted for dealing with the pulses and changes of the last half-century? Imagine what all the permutations of culture have done to them, how they have felt tossed about and bereft of familiar landmarks. It isn't any wonder that most of them feel bewildered, overwhelmed, even angry about the uncertainty of existence, or that many are holding onto their faith only by their fingertips.

Despite the Gallup Poll figures that continue to show high percentages of Americans who believe in God, pray with some regularity and think of themselves as moderately religious persons, it has been impossible for church members to live through the experiences of the last 50 years and not be deeply affected by increasing technicization and secularization, changing morality and lifestyles, galloping pluralism, and constant media attention to conflicting modes of belief and philosophy. When pressed individually to talk about their faith and understanding, many of those who began by saying they believe in God, Christ, and the church dissolve into confessions of uncertainty, doubt, and confusion, pleading with an air of helplessness, "What can a person believe in a world like ours?"

William Hinson, senior minister of First United Methodist Church in Houston, tells about the experience of his brother-in-law Miles when he was a boy taking piano lessons. Trained to locate middle "C" just beside the "W" on the family's Wurlitzer piano, he managed to learn one piece well enough to be included in the usual student recital. The evening of the recital, he strode confidently onto the stage, seated himself at the piano, then froze in horror. The piano was a Yamaha![5]

This is a metaphorical picture of where most people find themselves today. Familiar guidelines have given way to unfamiliar ones. Nothing seems to be what it was. The great cultural shift occurring in the world at large seriously affects the thinking of people in the most guarded citadels of faith and learning. Eventually it must overpower even the strongholds of conservatism and fundamentalism. Once the astronomers' telescopes were refined enough to discern what was really happening in the heavens, all the dogma in the world could not reverse the inevitable conclusion that the earth danced around the sun with the other planets, not the sun around the earth. There is always a time-lag for the absorbing of truth, and the more conservative the institution, the greater the delay; but truth will eventually work its way over, through, and around all barriers. Meanwhile, everybody is affected, albeit in varying degrees, by the changes being felt. We are all uneasy to find ourselves sitting at a Yamaha that was once a Wurlitzer.

How does the minister of a Christian church deal with this in his or her preaching? What are the hidden factors in parishioners' mindsets that must be taken into account in planning sermons and attempting to declare the gospel? Never mind that some churches appear to be doing well by ignoring the factors and proclaiming a traditionalist faith in an overloud voice; time will sort them out. The sensitive preacher, committed to effective ministry, will not wish to flail about blindly and ineptly in the pulpit, but wants to know as much about his or her listeners as possible, in order to preach as faithfully as possible.

What can we say about these listeners, based on the evidence of a massive cultural shift at the end of the twentieth century and the extensive literature it has produced? What are their feelings, hopes, fears, predilections, and sensibilities? Who are they, under the cosmeticized faces they present to the pulpit on Sunday mornings, and with what kinds of mental and emotional configurations are we attempting to interface when we frame our liturgies and craft our sermons?

The Hermeneutic Of Suspicion

Below the surface of their typical American hope and bravado, most of our parishioners are living with a measure of confusion, skepticism, and cynicism Americans have never before had to deal with. They hold on somewhat desperately to beliefs and traditions that they identify with a more solid and workable past, but they realize with an increasing sense of uneasiness that these beliefs and traditions are not only under siege but are, in many cases, actually disintegrating under the pressure of the new world being born. If it is true that reality for most of them is determined by the general experience, by what other persons attest to be true and reliable, then they cannot but be deeply affected by a certain wavering in the attestations these days. The sheer fact of the new pluralism in this country, with increasing attention being paid to the cultures of Jews, Muslims, and Buddhists no longer "out there" somewhere but here in our midst, is enough to unnerve many of those who always assumed that there was a bedrock American faith characterized by the church on the corner and Norman Rockwell's portraits of families bowing their heads over the Thanksgiving dinner.

As James Davison Hunter argues in *Culture Wars: The Struggle to Define America,* the cultural conflicts that have taken place over the better part of American history have taken place *within* the boundaries of a general culture that might be called biblical or traditional and which therefore provided a common ground for resolving the dispute. Now, in a secular world where religious pluralism is only a part of the problem we experience in trying to communicate with one another, there is no longer a common ground. We no longer address each other in the same language or with the same assumptions.[6]

Many people, in the welter of voices and opinions being recorded today, no longer know where to place their trust. It is as if the one reliable landscape of moral and theological teachings has become altogether chimerical, so that the most familiar residences of meaning and understanding frequently and unexpectedly give way to the slightest pressure.

As Robert Bellah and his colleagues attest in *The Good Society,* we all have profound misgivings about the majority of the very institutions that once defined our existence. Government has become a hopeless muddle of agencies and subagencies, all vying with one another for recognition and funding, and spinning whatever lies are necessary for self-perpetuation and aggrandizement. The courts have become tangled webs of suits and countersuits, laws and opinions, costs and delays, often rewarding sleaze and corruption while punishing truth and integrity and defying sensible attempts to disentangle or modify them in the direction of practical justice. Corporate life, that once responded more immediately to the general welfare and public opinion, has become so incredibly convoluted and esoteric that few people can keep up with its Byzantine workings, much less hold it morally and financially accountable. And the church, given its institutional sclerosis, the gap between leadership and laity, the highly publicized scandals of television preachers, and the general air of suspicion in which we now live our lives, sometimes seems little better than all the other failed or failing organizations.

In such a milieu, we are prone to feel an unhappy resonance for Eugene Ionesco's *The Chairs,* a tour de force of a play about an old man who has spent his entire life studying the great philosophies of the world and wants to impart the benefit of his wisdom before he dies. He and his wife invite dozens of important citizens to their room atop a lighthouse where they live, and set chairs out for them as they arrive. The guests are invisible, but the chairs proliferate until there is barely room for the old couple to move around. The last person to arrive is a professional orator, for the old man has not trusted his own powers of communication for this important occasion.

He introduces the orator, says that he has coached him in every detail of the message to be given, and then, with his wife, promptly leaps out the window. The orator, who has stood with his back to the audience, finally turns to speak. "Arrgh, geueeu, ugggh," he says. He is a mute, completely without the ability to speak.

Where indeed is the meaning of life? Is existence itself kaleidoscopic, with the patterns rearranging themselves every few centuries and sending shockwaves through all humanity when they do it?

What Can A Person Believe?

Religiously speaking, what it all comes down to is that many people aren't even sure what they can count on among their traditional beliefs. Higher criticism of the scriptures, academic investigation into the true history of the church, satirical treatments of religion by novelists and playwrights, Freudianism and the idea that God is merely a super father figure, Christendom's failure to respond adequately to the Holocaust and the Civil Rights movement, theological proclamations of the Death of God, the ignorance, greed, and lust of prominent television evangelists, the inability of noted theologians to agree on matters of faith, the growing pluralism of religious culture in America, burgeoning distrust of institutions, and now the collapse of civil religion and the desiccation of the mainstream churches have all taken a heavy toll on believers' confidence in their own faith-structures. Suppose nearly two millennia of church and theology have been a tremendous exercise in the manufacturing of illusion, a self-perpetuating, self-inflating myth that developed its own rationale and superstructures as the centuries passed.

I remember the reaction of a friend of mine, a businessman, upon reading about the Jesus Seminar, the group of scholars who meet annually to report on their investigations into particular sayings in the Gospels to determine whether Jesus did or did not actually say what has been attributed to him. "I can't even read the Beatitudes or the parables any more," he said, "without wondering if they are the sayings of an impostor, or, worse yet, of a group of impostors. It's as if I found out that my bank statements had all been invented by a committee of public relations people and had nothing to do with my real account."

The Gallup polls admittedly show little evidence of the erosion of faith in the U.S. Nine Americans in ten (actually, 94 percent) say they believe in God or a universal spirit. Seven in ten believe that God has "led or guided" them in making decisions in their lives. One in three believe that God has spoken to them in some direct fashion. Three in four believe that God has an actual plan for their lives, although they may not know what it is.[7] This sounds like a nation where faith is alive and well and living in the hearts of the people, not a nation smitten by disenchantment.

But there is no gainsaying the fact that life for all Americans has become increasingly secular, with the church playing less and less a role in people's personal schedules as well as in the public arena. When this happens, it is impossible for their confidence in faith and tradition to remain as strong as it formerly was. Trust in God and the dogmas of the church becomes subtly and surely eroded, so that personal belief is hollower and less substantive than it appears on the surface. There may be a clue in the Woody Allen film *Crimes and Misdemeanors* (there are always clues in Allen's films) when a character says of a woman she knows that she rejects the Bible because it has "a completely unbelievable central character." People today are concerned about what is believable and what is not. Doubt is more active at all levels of the intellectual processes than was once the case. The habit of empiricism is becoming less and less selective, so that it applies to religion as well as to other areas of life.

Lesslie Newbiggin, who since his retirement as Bishop of South India has assumed a leadership role on the world evangelical scene, has spoken repeatedly in his writings of the

Enlightenment as an enemy of faith. Most of the churches, he says, made alliances with the Enlightenment, altering doctrines and shifting ground where necessary in order to accommodate the new science and learning. Church leaders thought for two centuries that it was possible to welcome into their houses the discoveries of biology, geology, physics, and corresponding philosophies of science by broadening their theologies and shifting emphases to avoid the more obvious conflicts. Now, thinks Newbiggin, an empirical, secular attitude has come to prevail in the world and threatens to destroy Christians' beliefs in their own world view.

Reflecting this opinion, Stanley Hauerwas and William Willimon, in their book *Resident Aliens*,[8] have called for congregations of believers to create countercultural cells that consciously reject prevailing modern belief systems. Rejecting as pernicious H. Richard Niebuhr's image in *Christ and Culture* of "Christ Transforming Culture," because its criterion for a Christ-transformed culture merely affirms the kind of culture produced by liberal American Protestantism, they ask for colonies of believers oriented around the cross of Christ and prepared to signal alternative ways of life to the world. Christians are not naturally born, they say, but intentionally made. Cultural Christianity is coming to mean the death of Christianity as Jesus and his followers intended it. People *say* they believe in God, but their belief is actually shallow and nonspecific, and is easily swept away by personal or domestic crisis.

As a pastor, I was often privy to intimate conversations in which church members who had recently lost loved ones or undergone sudden reversals of fortune wondered whether their belief in God was really ill-founded, for everything in their personal experience conspired to make them feel that there was very little comfort in faith for the tremendous suffering they were experiencing. I remember one woman, the wife of a banker who had undergone public humiliation for his role in making some large investment loans that failed, who said she could not believe in a God who allowed her husband to be hurt as he was hurt and concluded that the very notion of a deity is something the church keeps alive merely to sustain its own place in the social framework. Later, when her husband had been completely exonerated of wrongdoing, she relented and became involved in church work again. But I am sure the taste of her unbelief lingers and often taints her present sense of faith.

From Boston To Las Vegas

One of the surest signs of the practical agnosticism of today's society, including society in the church, is the degree of relativism in both private and public morality. This is not a judgment on current moral practices; it is simply a recognition of the way those practices have tended to free-float for the past 30 years, assuming less and less reference to the moral precepts that governed both Judaism and Christianity for centuries. The divorce began to become most apparent, interestingly, during the mid-sixties and early seventies, at the very time when the church was being judged by the culture for its failure in the Civil Rights and anti-war movements. Regardless of whether there is a relationship between the two, moral standards in the U.S. have markedly changed in the last few decades.

Neil Postman, in *Amusing Ourselves to Death*, points out that the American character has often been symbolized by certain cities. In the late eighteenth century, Boston epitomized the spirit of freedom and decorum brought to these shores by the original settlers. By the mid-nineteenth century, New York had become the center of American vitality and the magnet for dreamers and the dispossessed from many lands. In the early twentieth century, Chicago stood as an image of the dynamic, preserving spirit of a nation of pioneers and doers. Now, says Postman, at the end of the twentieth century, we must look to Las Vegas, the city of lights, entertainment, sex, and gambling, as the symbol of our national aspirations.

"Las Vegas is a city entirely devoted to the idea of entertainment, and as such proclaims the spirit of a culture in which all public discourse increasingly takes the form of entertainment. Our politics, religion, news, athletics, education and commerce have been transformed into congenial adjuncts of show business, largely without protest or even much popular notice."[9]

Postman is not the only critic to suggest that our entire existence has been seduced by the need for entertainment. John Silber, former president of Boston University, says that our addiction to television has led us to seek pleasure wherever we can find it, whatever the consequences; and, because pleasure is by nature transient, the need for entertainment becomes insatiable and our lives are destined to be endlessly frustrated and unsatisfied.[10] Therefore we are always seeking the quick fix and the easy high — from sex, sports, violence, materialism, anything that will provide it.

Sports is an obvious example. As a nation, we have gone sports mad. A quick evening survey of television cable channels will usually turn up several ball games appropriate to the season, plus one or two channels devoting themselves to golf, car racing, or bowling. Herb Barks, former headmaster at Baylor School in Chattanooga, says that sports have become "far too important" in our existence. Eight out of ten parents who come to his office are there not to inquire about scholastic matters or whether their children are developing as well balanced human beings but to talk about their children and sports.

"Winning is everything," says Barks, " — for the coach, for the player, for the school. We may talk about other things, but if you keep on losing, you are going to find out that winning is the key. So it is an immoral system. Immoral because it hurts kids. It is not just a few bad parts in a big system, it's a big bad system that hurts kids in order to provide a bored and often apathetic generation with entertainment."[11]

Barks sees our preoccupation with sports as part of the moral rot of our national fibre. We glorify beef and brawn, power and prowess, at the expense of art, wit, humor, intelligence, goodness, kindness, love, and other human virtues. We inculcate a philosophy of winning over a spirit of serving. We idolize strength and endurance over gentleness and relationship. We fritter away our national energy and resources on pastimes, on entertainment, when we should be trying to build a better world where the hungry are fed, the ill receive medical treatment, and impoverished nations are supported and nurtured by the wealthier ones.

What kind of church are Saturday's most ardent football fans likely to attend on Sunday? Probably not a quiet, reflection-oriented mainline church where people sing traditional hymns and the minister preaches gentle, thoughtful sermons. They are much more likely to select a congregation where the action is fast-paced, a strong personality directs the public singing, the choir is filled with attractive younger men and women, and the preacher is an obvious extrovert who devotes 20 percent of his (!) sermon time to reflecting on yesterday's game. In other words, they will choose a church with obvious sex appeal.

And speaking of sex, few things have changed more in the last 30 years than public attitudes toward individual sexual behavior. Since the sixties, our society seems to have become virtually unshockable. We see frontal nudity on television, watch x-rated films, hire strippers for office parties, quote Masters and Johnson at the dinner table, give sex instruction to grade schoolers, hand out condoms on street corners, applaud grandma when she repeats words she's heard from Sophia on *Golden Girls*, and have Sunday morning sermons on God, sex, and the liberal mindset.

One of the most blatant exploitations of sex in our culture is for advertising. Attractive men and seductive women tout cars, colognes, soaps, breakfast cereals, pantyhose, vaginal creams, wines, pet foods, and almost everything else. They become part of the general hype of the culture, a culture of doublespeak, overspeak, and extraspeak, where PR, the "spin," the "gyre," hyping a product, has become as familiar as water in the tap or a carpet on the floor. Universal huckstering has brought us to the point where few of us really believe anything any more, where promotional ads for trucks, civic events, political candidates, churches, and giveaways are all taken *cum grano salis*, with an appropriate skepticism born of misrepresentation and oversell. Even children soon develop a certain distrust of the bright, attractive world being offered them on television ads, for the ads invariably inflate the quality and value of what they sell.

It doesn't take a genius to see what this does to the credibility of a religious faith based primarily on words, testimonies, and sermons. The intelligent young person hears a minister make a statement about the benefit of discipleship and thinks, almost unconsciously, that religion is as overblown as almost everything else in the world.

What the ads *do* sell to an unwitting public is a consumerist mentality based on entertainment, self-gratification, and sheer materialism. While specific claims about products put off wary buyers, the ads tend to create a climate of luxuriance and self-indulgence that affects the public psyche and benefits commercialism in general. They keep America wanting and buying, and this fuels the engine of the national economy. They also undermine the Christian ethic, which, as Gabriel Marcel put it years ago in his book, *Being and Having*, is really aimed at being something, not at having things. People whose chief aim in life is having things, he said, end by being possessed by their possessions. Only those who have discovered their relationship to God and, in that discovery, need nothing else are truly free. All the others are indentured to the culture and the times.

Specifically, how does all this affect the people who sit in our pews on Sunday morning? The tension in their lives is easy to imagine. They come to church to worship in the name of a man who plainly rejected wealth and comfort for the sake of a free spirit and a humble relationship to God; yet they have come, for the most part, in Hondas, Buicks, and BMWs, and are thinking about interest rates, pay raises, and IRAs. They hear sermons about how hard it is for the rich to get into heaven; yet they are concerned about how to get their children into the best schools and colleges and how to move to a better home or apartment. They wear their best clothes and have their hair smoothly lacquered; yet they feel bored out of their minds and wish they were at a movie or a ballgame. They mouth the hymns and bow their heads for prayers; yet they wonder how much of it is really true and whether they are not helping to perpetuate a public fantasy by coming to church at all.

Facing A Closed Future

The truth is, there is more depression among churchgoers today than there has probably ever been in the history of Christianity. There is a lot of depression in the culture as a whole. Psychologists remark on it all the time. But the fact that there is as much depression in the church as there is in the world outside the church is merely another sign that the kind of Christianity we have become used to, public or civil Christianity, is the kind most people in the churches know and that it is inadequate for dealing with life in this era of massive culture shift.

The age of mental depression in America began at the same time when national ideals were fading and Protestantism was beginning to collapse, in the 1960s. Significantly, it was the time when drugs were first seriously introduced to American culture and the DEA became an important government agency. American young people, led by Harvard professor Timothy Leary, learned to "tune in and drop out," popping pills and smoking marijuana to escape the legacy of work, rectitude, and responsibility that had typically passed from generation to generation before them.

One of the brightest young novelists of the era, Richard Brautigan, captured the spirit of the time in stories about world-weary hippies who hitchhiked across the country, lived in castoff clothing, learned to beg for coins on streetcorners, and huddled together in communes where they smoked pot, sang anti-war songs, and confessed that they were orphans in a world gone awry. Brautigan's novel *Confederate General from Big Sur* opens with a scene in Franklin Park in San Francisco, where the statue of Benjamin Franklin, inventor, author, framer of a nation, stands now looking toward the East, back to where the experience of American nationality began, and presides over a park filled with dropouts and protesters wearing Indian beads, strumming guitars, and passing reefers to one another. The irony can hardly be missed. The great Westward migration is over. The pioneers have scrambled across the plains, the rivers, and the mountains, all the way to the Pacific, and now there is no more frontier, nowhere else to go. The nation must turn back on itself, survey the way it has come. The future will be different from the past. Huck Finn has grown up to become Ernest Hemingway, who discharged a shotgun in his mouth.

Brautigan realized what many of us took longer to see, that since the fulfillment of Manifest Destiny there has been no place where we can escape the perils and complications of civilization. Now, since World War II and Korea and Vietnam, and with the exposure of our nerve system in the Civil Rights and anti-war movements, there is no easy future for us to dream about, no Nirvana around the corner or Shangri-La over the next hill. Suddenly the Golden Age is no longer ahead of us; now it lies somewhere in the past, in the time of our colonization or the robust era of industrialization or the long period of the public church, when life and the national purpose and public morality appeared all to be unified and moving in the same direction. Today, when nothing seems to work any more, the economy is in a slump, infrastructures are deteriorating, education is faltering, illiteracy is growing, Protestantism is disintegrating, and monstrous criminality is destroying our cities, we long for the good old days, for peace and prosperity and purpose. Come to think of it, we would even settle for prosperity and purpose.

The people who come to our churches now are quite possibly the most stressed, overworked, and generally unhappy people churches have ever seen. The very fact that they live in a time of cultural transformation is mentally and emotionally exhausting to them. The simple world of their parents' traditions has exploded in every direction. A nation of manageable cities, clearly separated from one another by rural land and joined by roads that ran by farms, trees, villages, and country stores, has given way to great, indistinguishable metropolitan areas with broad interstate highways, vast warehouse areas, impersonal housing units, and dangerous slums. Families that once spent evenings and weekends together, took in ill or indigent relatives, and had clear lines of authority and responsibility have disintegrated into quicksilvery globules that dart unpredictably here and there with little true relationship to one another. Cultural ideals that once included Sunday school and church attendance, backyard gardens, neighborhood schools, block parties, sandlot ballgames, Saturday housecleanings, long courtships, and big Sunday dinners have lost out to professional sports, wide-screen television, seven-day-a-week shopping malls, traffic jams, sex on request, and computerized checkout systems. People feel out of control of their lives and environments. They are confused about how a faith of shepherds and tentmakers fits in a world of rock stars and microchips. "Peace" is just a word to them. They have forgotten how to imagine what it really is.

The Fallout For Ministers

So what happens? For one thing, people feel resentful toward life, toward God, toward the church, toward whatever higher power or greater entity caused or permitted them to be thrust out of the warm cocoon of the past into the terrifying speed and experience of their present situation. They may not know they are resentful. They haven't been to a psychiatrist and talked about it. But down under their apparently confident and self-reliant exteriors, they feel it. It seeps and drips and oozes and seethes, and occasionally vents itself in sighs and yells and cranky attitudes when everything seems too heavy or too much and they're not sure they can carry on any longer.

And by extension they are also resentful toward their pastors, the ministers of their churches, who, more than anyone else in the tangible world of everyday relationships, represent God and the erstwhile stability of church and tradition to them. Nothing else is sufficient to explain the rash of minister-bashing that has spread like an epidemic through Christian churches in recent years. Pastoral firings are up dramatically in the last decade. Ministers report increased and often irrational pressure from their boards and lay leaders. Hate letters, snide remarks, refusals to raise pay or repair parsonages, are all part of a barrage of insults and signs of a general depreciation of the ministers' services.

One denominational official told me that his office noticed a sudden upswing in conflicts between congregations and pastors in the spring of 1986. It was not connected to anything in particular, as far as the official could tell. Prior to that year, he said, his office was usually deluged during the Lenten season by cries of ministers needing help with problems in their churches. Characteristically, the cries would fall off after Lent, presumably when the pressures of the season died away and the ministers had more time to deal with whatever situations had arisen. That year, in 1986, they didn't fall off. Nor have they abated since.

The stories of members' attitudes toward their pastors are legion. A few will suffice to suggest their occasional viciousness.

The minister of a large Baptist church in Alabama was targeted for destruction by members of his congregation after he influenced the church's mission committee to designate a portion of their annual funds to help churches in Eastern Europe (these members wished all the funds to continue to go through their denomination's so-called Cooperative Program, so that the church would get credit for huge gifts to the program). They created so much dissension in the church that the minister could not concentrate on preparing original sermons on Sunday and began occasionally to borrow the sermons of other ministers. Discovering the source of one of these borrowed sermons, the dissenters got a local newspaper to print the minister's sermon side-by-side with the original, displaying slavish copying and embarrassing both the church and the minister.

The wife of a United Methodist minister in a small town in Indiana was smitten by a stroke that caused total paralysis. At first, the congregation responded warmly and lovingly, expressing sympathy and bringing casseroles to the parsonage. Within a few months, however, the people began to murmur about having a "helpless" pastor's wife who demanded more of the minister's attention than they wished to share. The bishop of the conference ignored their protests and kept the minister there, but the unhappiness became so vocal and relentless that the minister finally had to request a transfer. He said he could not live with the hate and dissension his wife's condition was engendering in the people.

A Disciples of Christ church in Tennessee called a new minister who had a mentally retarded daughter. Shortly before the minister and his wife moved to the field, they requested that the parsonage committee permit them to paint the rooms of the parsonage in different colors, so that their daughter, who was used to a similar arrangement where they lived, could more easily distinguish among them. The committee, which had expressed active dislike for two previous ministers and their families, responded negatively, saying that they did not expect the new minister's family to be there long enough to make such an arrangement practical.

A United Methodist minister in Southern California was experiencing constant criticism from a few couples in his church. One particular complaint involved the fact that he was responsible for overseeing the custodians' work and that Sunday school teachers often found their rooms untidy when they entered on Sunday mornings. One Saturday night, an associate pastor who had forgotten to take home some papers she needed to review before Sunday stopped by the church to get them. She noticed lights on in the building and approached cautiously, looking in the window before entering. Inside, some of the ministers' critics were busily disturbing furniture arrangements, messing up blackboards, and scattering debris on the floor.

These are only random cases and prove little in themselves. But they are indicative of the kinds of stories one hears over and over from ministers in recent years, suggesting a general change in the attitudes most congregations once had toward their ministers. There have always been church members who were unhappy with their ministers, and members who were unkind or even vicious in their behavior. But what is different today is the extraordinary prevalence of the phenomenon. As the situation for Protestantism in general has worsened, the existence of coteries of church members anxious to attack or even persecute their ministers has become almost epidemic.

Someone has perceptively likened the situation of the average minister to that of a football coach. As long as the team is winning and things are going well, he or she is well liked and safe. But the minute things go the other way and the team begins to lose games, complaints begin. If the losses don't stop, the complaints worsen, and eventually reach the level where a personnel change is demanded. Unfortunately, ministers don't usually have pay-out contracts like those of coaches, and their families often suffer inordinately from the unkindness of church members.

Reluctance To Make Commitments

Another characteristic of many church members today is that they are extremely hesitant to commit themselves and their energies to the church with the kind of passionate dedication necessary to effect important changes in the church's make-up. Mary Ann Glendon (in *Rights Talk*) and Robert Bellah and his colleagues (in *The Good Society*) are right, the nature of individualism is so rich and all-demanding today that people

67

rarely give themselves to institutions or organizations with the kind of wholeheartedness institutions and organizations once enjoyed and continue to need. There is always the reservation, Well-I'll-do-what-I-can-but-my-time-is-very-limited, as if the person cannot afford to get engaged in anything that might require real pain or sacrifice.

What if the church, after all, is wrong? What if it doesn't prove to be fulfilling to the member's self? What if the member ceases to like the minister or is out of town too much to participate fully or decides that a neighboring church is better? Better to be undercommitted than overcommitted.

Norman Neaves, pastor of Oklahoma City's Church of the Servant, tells about a man who attended his church for years and always sat behind some large green plants at the rear of the sanctuary. When Norman met him one day and expressed surprise, the man explained that he didn't really want to get involved, so he always slipped in after the service began and sat there out of sight. I believe Norman said he is a psychiatrist.

Most ministers know the story only too well. The members of their congregations may not enter late and hide behind plants, but a majority of them are almost as slippery when it comes to trying to get them involved in the daily life and work of the church. Their litany of excuses is long and imaginative: they work too many hours a week, they can't come out at night, they have to keep themselves free in case their children or parents need them, they hyperventilate when they have to attend meetings, they are prone to anxiety dreams, they had a bad experience once in another church, they want to keep their relationship to the church on a "spiritual" level, they don't feel worthy of serving, they feel too bad to serve, their eyesight is failing, they have a lot of doctor's appointments, and on and on.

A man in Los Angeles sent me a note saying he had liked my sermon on Sunday morning and was enclosing a check for $100. I wrote him a word of thanks. He replied and said: "Don't get any ideas. I sent $100 to the California Atheists' Club as well. I believe in keeping my options open."

I think that remark was meant to be humorous, but it expresses what a lot of people appear to feel. They don't want to get involved. They don't even like to sign the guest book at the church they attend, lest someone get their phone number or address and try to contact them about membership or responsibilities. They prefer to remain anonymous, to slip in and out without being caught, without being buttonholed to contribute or solicited to become meaningful parts of the whole. They are like hummingbirds sipping nectar here and there without lighting while they do it. In their highly transient world, they don't want to risk growing any roots or being obligated to stay anywhere for very long.

As a result, most of the churches in mainline Protestantism remain under the control of a few old-timers, people who have been in the congregations long enough to outlast several pastors and a lot of temporary members, and these old-timers develop a sense of ownership that tends to repel newcomers. They begin to think of the churches as their private domains, as businesses they run for their own benefit, and they resent the occasional intruder who is bold enough to stand for office or make suggestions about how "their" church ought to be managed. They become more concerned about what kind of manure to spread around their rosebushes than about the real mission of the church, which is to worship God, preach the gospel, and reach out in compassion to the multitudes.

Everybody loses. The people who are reluctant to become involved lose, because they never discover the joy of give-and-take in a real world, never mingle their tears with the tears of others, never know the commanding presence of Christ in the fellowship of a local, particular congregation. The old-timers lose, because they live with an incomplete notion of the church and have only a truncated experience of congregational life; they remain "in charge," but miss the thrill and reward of being part of a movement where they could have been caught up in the real life of the Spirit, inundated by waves of transcendent power and demand. And the church as a whole loses, for it fails to reach its true potential and never becomes a dynamic locus of intersection for the holy and the human, the local and the universal, the immediate and the eternal.

Wolfhart Pannenberg says in *Christian Spirituality* that the absolute freedom of the individual in modern life, so highly regarded by most people, often leaves people enormously lonely and unrelated to anything that might prove inspiring and redemptive. "It is not likely," he says, "that secular societies will be able in the long run to survive the consequences of the much-touted emancipation of the individual."[12]

Nor will the church, we might add. It too requires commitment to survive.

What Do You Say To A Naked Man?

Confusion and cynicism, skepticism about religious beliefs, relativism in morality, depression about the future, resentment toward God and ministers, reluctance to become involved in the life and mission of a congregation — these are hard, negative judgments about the people who still come to our churches in the era of the Protestant debacle.

Are they justified?

Not about all church members, surely. We leap instinctively and immediately to the defense of the saints we know who continue to display Christlike demeanor and attend to the work of the congregation. They seem to exist almost as anachronisms today, genuine Christians who undergo constant conversion to the spirit of the gospel and live without pretension or false piety in the face of all the problems confronting the church in our time. Like Mother Teresa, they go about their duties with simple, uncalculating commitment, fresh every day from their morning devotions and an abiding conviction (with apologies to Robert Browning) that God's in her heaven and everything will be all right with the world.

But how many of the people in the pews on Sunday morning are described by this encomium? Twenty percent? Ten percent? Five percent? The truth is that most of the people who visit our churches and hear our sermons on a given Sunday morning are at least partially, if not largely, reflected in what I have described in this chapter. They are not bad people. They are not trying to run from God. On the contrary, they are basically good people and they want to discover how to let God take charge of their lives. But they live in an increasingly secularistic environment where life has changed dramatically in the last 25 years and they are often puzzled, frightened, dismayed, and depressed by their circumstances. They don't come to church because they've got everything together. They come because they *don't* have it together, because they're looking for something, because they're vaguely hoping they may find it in church, because they remember that church is where it was once possible to find it and they have the right instincts in coming back to look for it there.

"What do you say to a naked man who approaches you in the middle of Times Square bearing a large fish?"

That was a question someone drew in a classroom game called "What Do You Say?" It is very nearly the question facing us preachers today: What do you say to a person in your congregation who comes to you basically bereft of the ways and traditions that once made life meaningful and the journey manageable? What do you emphasize? How do you frame your statements? What do you include and what do you leave out? How do you communicate when most of the old symbols are dead?

This is the stuff of our next chapter.

How are we supposed to preach the gospel in an age when the waters roar and are troubled, when the mountains rise up and fall into the sea?

---

1. Langdon Gilkey, "A Retrospective Glance at My Work," in Donald W. Musser and Joseph L. Price, eds., *The Whirlwind in Culture: Frontiers in Theology* (Bloomington, Indiana: Morris-Stone Books, 1988), p. 20.

2. Langdon Gilkey, *Naming The Whirlwind* (Indianapolis: Bobbs-Merrill, 1969).

3. Langdon Gilkey, *Religion and the Scientific Future* (New York: Harper and Row, 1970).

4. Langdon Gilkey, *Creationism on Trial: Evolution and God in Little Rock* (Minneapolis: Winston Press, 1985).

5. William Hinson, *A Place to Dig In* (Nashville: Abingdon Press, 1987), pp. 13-14.

6. James Davison Hunter, *Culture Wars: The Struggle to Define America* (New York: HarperCollins Basic Books, 1991), p. 42.

7. Gallup and Castelli, *The People's Religion,* pp. 71-72.

8. Stanley Hauerwas and William Willimon, *Resident Aliens* (Nashville: Abingdon Press, 1989).

9. Neil Postman, *Amusing Ourselves to Death: Public Discourse in the Age of Show Business* (New York: Viking, 1985), pp. 3-4.

10. John Silber, *Straight Shooting: What's Wrong With America and How to Fix It* (New York: Harper and Row, 1989), p. 69.

11. Herb Barks, *Reading the River* (Nashville: Abingdon Press, 1987), p. 140.

12. Wolfhart Pannenberg, *Christian Spirituality* (Philadelphia: Westminster Press, 1983), pp. 189-190.

Chapter 3

Preaching In The Last Days Of The Mainline Church

Tom Troeger, in *The Parable of Ten Preachers,* tells the story of a United Methodist minister, Jason Kirk, who pastors the local church in a village named Clydes Corners. Clydes Corners was established at the turn of the century by a successful farmer whose name was Cedric Clyde. The same gentleman also paid off the indebtedness of the church and donated a massive red horsehair couch that has ever since dominated the chancel of said church.

Newer, younger members who have moved into the area detest the couch as a symbol of tastelessness and vulgarity, and would like nothing better than to relegate it to the dump heap. But the older members refuse to hear of its removal, for, in their way of thinking, it unites them with their traditions and the days of a greater sanity in the world.

"Let me tell you about proclaiming the gospel into the twenty-first century in Clydes Corners," says Jason Kirk. "I stand in that pulpit, and over here, down to the right, sits the Clyde family. All of them. And over here in the middle sit the ones who don't care, and over there, front left and back left, sit the new families. And every sentence I put in the air I see them all weighing whether it is ammunition for their side or the other side. Here I am preaching about the love of God, and everything I say is filtered through a single question: Is the pastor in favor of the red horsehair couch, or is the pastor against the red horsehair couch? I regret to say that is what preaching toward the twenty-first century in Clydes Corners has come to be."[1]

Many pastors, I suspect, will readily identify with this fictional clergyman. Their churches have their own versions of the red horsehair couch. Their congregations are almost fatally divided over issues and objects that seem entirely irrelevant to the gospel of Jesus Christ. In some churches, the conflict is over how the congregations will respond to changing conditions in their neighborhoods or communities: Will they open their doors to peoples of different races and backgrounds, seeking to find new life through sharing and serving, or will they insulate themselves more fiercely against the shifting tides and remain as they are until they die? Will they permit local gangs to play basketball in their parking lot, and place portajohns on the lot for the use of the homeless, or will they vigorously police the property and expel intruders? In other churches, the conflict is over mundane physical matters: Should they repoint the bricks in the building, paint the sanctuary a soft, new color, hang vibrant banners over the cracks in the chancel, replace the largely dysfunctional old organ, tear out the asbestos jacket of the aging boiler, purchase a new audio system, put hearing aids in the pews, or substitute the denomination's most recent hymnals for the dog-eared volumes that now adorn the racks?

To many of us, the management of such conflicts among local congregations amounts to little more than rearranging the deck chairs on the *Titanic*. In the larger view of things, they can have little consequence. But to the church members caught up in the conflicts, they are usually matters of life and death, or at least of success and failure. Their perspectives have been allowed to atrophy and narcissize to the point where they no longer view things *sub specie aeternitatis* or *sub specie crucis;* instead, they view everything as a contest of will and authority, and see themselves as guardians of truth and correctness in a world gone awry.

In the words of W. H. Auden,

> *[They] would rather be ruined than changed,*
> *[They] would rather die in [their] dread*
> *Than climb the cross of the moment*
> *And let [their] illusions die.*[2]

It is of course impossible to say how much of the conflictual nature of local churches is natural human cussedness and nothing new at all (we mustn't forget Paul's Corinthian correspondence), but it is easy to believe, on the other hand, that this nature has been sorely aggravated in recent years by the enormity of the cultural shift and corresponding personal and mass confusion we have alluded to in the previous chapters. People do tend to be more irritable and less forgiving when they are psychologically stressed and unable to communicate with their own centers than when they are enjoying peace and fullness in their inner beings. Sociologists have even suggested that nations behave more truculently in the family of nations during periods of social and economic unrest within their own borders. It is reasonable to expect, therefore, that congregations in a time of great cultural transition will be more agitated and restless, and will have more difficulty focusing and agreeing on the central issues of the faith, than the same congregations in periods of relative tranquility and continuity.

But what about preaching in an age of change and upheaval? For many, it is doubtless a more uncertain and difficult business than it has been for generations. There were several centuries, between the Reformation era and our own time, when all a minister had to do to be "successful" was to cast his or her lot (there were very few women) with a particular sect or denomination, commit to heart the doctrines and ways of the group, and then design and preach sermons that amplified reasonably well that body of teachings and traditions.

In the heyday of the industrial age, when literacy was probably at its zenith in western culture, this formula produced a line of great "princes of the pulpit" such as Phillips Brooks and Henry Ward Beecher in America and, in Britain, F. W. Robertson, Charles H. Spurgeon, R. W. Dale, Joseph Parker, G. Campbell Morgan, and Alexander Maclaren. Even as late as the twentieth century the church was still enjoying the "royalty" of such preachers as Harry Emerson Fosdick, George A. Buttrick, Paul E. Scherer, George W. Truett, Wallace Hamilton, Clovis Chappell, Theodore Ferris, Edmund Steimle, Leslie Weatherhead, Herbert H. Farmer, and James Stewart.

With the coming of a new age and the breakup of the old traditions, however, being a preacher in the mainline churches no longer entails what it once entailed. Congregations are no longer monolithic in membership, with all the members growing up in the same traditions and having the same expectations about ministry. Now there is no congregational consensus about what constitutes either good ministry or good preaching. There are almost as many sets of expectations as there are members in the congregations. People are not nourished by their traditions. They have an amazing ignorance about the Bible, church doctrine, sacramental mystery, denominational history, everything that once provided cohesion and direction for local churches. Their world has become flat, immediate, and devoid of clarifying references. While people still employ some of the old language, they do not begin to comprehend its heritage or nuances. Their ministers often feel like Jean-Baptiste Clamence, the narrator of Albert Camus' *The Fall*, who, speeding along in a motorboat in a thick fog on the Zuyder Zee, knows he is making progress but can see no landmarks and doesn't know if it's in the right direction. They despair, like Jason Kirk, of sounding any clear note of the gospel when everyone filters their sermons according to whether they are "for" or "against" the red horsehair couch.

How does the serious pastor approach the problems of preaching in an age of cultural reformation? What can he or she say that will make a difference in the lives of congregants facing the dissolution of their ecclesiastical doctrines and traditions, not to mention the total transformation of their culture and its relevant symbolisms?

This is an enormously difficult question, and one that must be answered only tentatively and in great humility. It would be unforgivably hubristic to pretend to know the answers in any definitive way, for the answers to such questions in times of dislocation and restructuring evolve organically out of the situation and do not always yield themselves to unerring forecast. Part of the problem in making the transition from one cultural epoch to another is that energy invariably assumes some forms that were unpredictable from the former vantage point, and we are better prepared for a new era when we simply expect this to be the case.

Yet it seems to me not too presumptuous to reach at least some tentative conclusions about the general thrust of Christian preaching in a time like ours. Thomas Klise, the novelist, spoke in *The Last Western* of "hints" and "lesser hints," and perhaps that is how these conclusions should be categorized, all of them as "hints" and some as "lesser" than others. But, if I were addressing a mainline congregation today, there are certain directions I would invariably take in my preaching, certain themes I would consistently sound, certain emphases I would return to again and again, as having recommended themselves to me both by their centrality to the faith of the earliest Christians and by their inescapable relevance in an age of upheaval and uncertainty.

In a general sense, I think I did tend to propound these themes during my more recent days in the parish, for I can find frequent echoes of them in the sermons I preached then. But if I were to return to the parish today I can assure the reader that I would announce them with far greater intentionality and intensity, for I sincerely believe them to be of utmost importance in transmitting the gospel of Christ from an era when we were more certain of its meaning — indeed, when we were more certain of everything — to an era when the meaning is less certain and yet inexpressibly rich with possibility.

Preaching For Clarification

First, I believe it is extremely important for preachers today to make huge efforts patiently to clarify for their parishioners the real nature of the culture shift we are in and how it affects their faith and their church, and to do so from the most comprehensive biblical and cultural positions it is possible to occupy. People are hungry for understanding. They are not merely sheep without shepherds, they are sheep in a wilderness area where there are no fences or sheepfolds, where there are wild beasts in every draw and behind every outcropping of rocks, and where the earth roars and shifts every few minutes with a devastating new quake. They are more desperate for information and overviews of the situation than even they are aware. Many of them have simply lost faith, not only in God but in life and the future, because they cannot assimilate or make sense of the radical changes affecting their lives today.

And who but the preacher has the kind of eschatological overview they need? Anthropologists have an overview; it focuses on human development since the time of the earliest skeletons found in Africa. But it hardly provides a sense of ultimate meaning for life. Biologists and physicians have an overview; it has to do with genes and chromosomes and the ability of human or nonhuman bodies to achieve wellness and functionality. But it does not really extend to the life of the mind and the feelings of the heart. Sociologists have an overview; it looks at social entities such as the individual and the group and studies how they interact under varying conditions at different times. But it fails to deal with the deepest human issues of faith, hope, and love. Psychologists and psychoanalysts have an overview; it examines the way individual selves cope with the facts and impressions of their environments and evolve into new selves containing the seeds or nucleus of the old. But it offers no understanding of the self in light of a God who lovingly created the world and its processes, and who yet tenderly guides those processes toward some distantly glorious and only partially adumbrated goal. Only the preacher standing in the Judeo-Christian tradition can speak meaningfully of creation, sin, and redemption, of wilderness wanderings and a city not made by human hands, of divine teleology, of the *meaning* of life and history and what happens to us individually and collectively when we go through a seismic shift of the kind we are presently experiencing. Only the preacher can talk about God and transcendence and the quality of inward journeys.

I said that people long for the kind of overview that only the preacher can provide. This is why *The Late Great Planet Earth* by Hal Lindsey was, outside the Bible itself, the best-selling book for the decade of the 1980s, outstripping, despite its millenarian sensationalism, immature philosophy, and shoddy biblicism, all detective stories, steamy sex novels, and serious pieces of literature. It purported to offer a truthful biblical overview, a schema for things that were happening in the world at the time, a template for understanding such disparate but pertinent matters as Communism, the Cold War, unrest in the Middle East, rising materialism in the West, and the apparent indifference of many Christians to the fate of the world and its civilization. In a world of sleaze, crime, war, nuclear power, drugs, rock concerts, and wasted lives, it promised an interpretation of what was happening, why God was permitting it to happen, and what God was supposedly going to do about it. People read and reread it, marked up their copies, shared them with friends, quoted it in office conversations, and treated it as having quasi-biblical status, all because it gave them a much needed handle, albeit a false one, on the tumultuous history of the last half of the twentieth century.

One reason for *The Late Great Planet Earth's* amazing success in the bookstores is the abysmal failure of the Christian pulpit generally to provide the kind of overall guidance and interpretation people need for making it through such cataclysmic times. Most of us preachers were too near the trees to see the forest. We were dealing with so many nickel-and-dime items among our parishioners that we couldn't see the ten-dollar issues. We were so busy trying to adapt to new liturgical usages, mediate among musical styles, treat broken marriages and lonely singles, understand changing sexual mores, design more comprehensive programs of Christian education, learn better counseling techniques, integrate churches and community services, develop soup kitchens and housing projects, become lectionary preachers with narrative sermons, avoid burnout, practice zero-based budgeting, and generally move our churches into the age of the computer and the word processor that we almost totally failed to step back, get the larger picture of what was happening to us and our people, and make that a part of our message. Diffident by nature and overwhelmed by the enormity of our jobs, we defaulted on our obligations and left it to the Hal Lindseys, Ron Hubbards, and Frank Perettis to draw the charts, describe the options, and draft the battleplans by which millions of Christians would live at the end of the most baffling century the world has probably ever seen.

Now it is important for us to recover our function as interpreters of history and culture. With the Bible in one hand and the morning newspaper in the other, as Karl Barth put it, we must enjoin once more the prophetic role of those who stand with Christ in the unfolding of the ages, and speak with a proper mixture of restraint and urgency, faith and intelligence, love and critical insight to parishioners being swept wildly about by current events and "every wind of doctrine."

Perhaps we couldn't do it before because we didn't see clearly enough what is happening on a global scale. Stuck in traffic on the freeway, we couldn't see the miles and miles of cars, trucks, and vans stretching in every direction, or understand how an accident five miles away was affecting our progress on our own little stretch of highway. But now we are beginning to see. Sociologists, economists, scientists, psychologists, educators, futurologists, and scholars from many disciplines are amassing the kind of data that enable us to discern trends and understand the patterns of what is going on in the world. Before, things were happening too quickly for us to absorb or comprehend them. Now we can at least tell the direction of flow, and see how many of the things that are happening are really interrelated instead of being discrete occurrences.

If we will only come up long enough from our immersion in immediate parish responsibilities to read the seminal thinkers and writers of our time, and begin to understand the implications of their works, we can see the relevance of what they are doing to the theology of the church and to the way we go about the task of being faithful to Christ in our everyday lives and work. They are providing the tools which, in conjunction with our knowledge of scripture and human nature, will enable us to delineate for our parishioners the outlines of human existence and the prospects for faithful Christian living in this new age.

As ministers, we should be reading books like Robert Reich's *The Next American Frontier,* Mary Ann Glendon's *Abortion and Divorce in American Law,* Michael Perry's *Law, Morality and Politics,* Jurgen Habermas' *The Structural Transformation of the Public Sphere,* Derek Bok's *Higher Learning,* Robert Wuthnow's *The Restructuring of American Religion,* John Kenneth Galbraith's *The New Industrial State,* Orio Giarini's *The Emerging Service Economy,* H. A. Raymond's *Management in the Third Wave,* Neil Postman's *Amusing Ourselves to Death,* John Silber's *Straight Shooting,* and Stephen Carter's *The Culture Of Disbelief.* This will give us a sense of confidence when conversing with the public about the world we live in and what it is becoming. Journals such as *Daedalus, The Christian Scholar, Atlantic Monthly, Forbes, Christianity and Crisis, First Things, Christian Century,* and *The New York Times Book Review* will likewise help us to keep abreast of the best that is being thought in the contemporary world and enable us to begin to make summary judgments about the movement of thought and events in the global arena. And for those with any compatibility with media, the eclectic journal *Wired* is a fantastic compendium of insights, ideas, and information.

At the same time, we should be immersing ourselves in the best in theological reflection, biblical studies, organizational theory, and pastoral care, so that we can hold in creative tension the world of religion and the world at large. It is important that the two spheres be bound in such tension; otherwise we tend to become either secularist gurus with no redemptive overview or spiritualist commentators with no real understanding of the milieu where our people live and work. One of the considerable problems with the conservative-fundamentalist movement of the past 20 years has been its hubristic one-sidedness, its attempt to make unilateral pronouncements about everything from international politics to women's rights to the nature of pornography without paying any attention to the evolution of human experience. As the only religious voice with a note of self-confidence, it has fared all too well with a large segment of the populace. But its judgments have struck most people of sense and sensibility as faulty and immature, like the ill-considered opinions of backwoods prophets and small-town demagogues. It is time we had some more Reinhold Niebuhrs and Robert McAfee Browns, deeply Christian personalities immersed in culture, politics, economics, literature, and religion, and thus able to speak with a fullness of vision and note of true authority the world will recognize. Every minister, in fact, ought to aspire to become a miniature Niebuhr or Brown, so steeped in the politics of daily life in the world that his or her word, when filtered through the pericopes of the sacred text, instantly creates new vistas for parishioners of what the world, under God, can be.

As for pericopes, there are plenty of them in the scope of the entire Bible that provide opportunities for the thoughtful minister to begin shaping rejuvenated worldviews for his or her congregation. Genesis opens with creation stories that are perfect introductions to discussions of the creative spirit, the relations of men and women, the use of raw materials, concern for the environment, and the relationship of work to leisure. In the latter part of Genesis there are wonderful bases for discussions of men/women issues, familial and tribal organization, and international relations. Exodus, Leviticus, Numbers, and Deuteronomy are filled with texts dealing with the moral basis of existence, interpersonal obligations, and the whole question of societal organization, as well as with ways of acknowledging the Holy in our midst and transmitting faith from generation to generation. The history books — 1 and 2 Samuel, 1 and 2 Chronicles, and 1 and 2 Kings — sparkle with stories about politics, society, the treatment of enemies, national goals, and the spotted realities of human existence. The many books of the prophets, from Isaiah and Jeremiah to Jonah and Amos and Hosea, overflow with material about compassion, justice, international relationships, and God's plan for the entire world. The Gospels, replete with stories about race, sex, poverty, illness, oppression, and the divine rule, cry out for first place in our repertoire of sermons. Acts and the Pauline letters are not far behind. And even the book of Revelation, with its sweeping portraits of religion and politics, offers almost countless possibilities for sermons about the coming world order and the judgment of God.

If the intelligent and highly educated ministers of the mainstream churches have left the preaching of this powerful book to the prejudiced, ill-informed, and semi-literate pastors of the religious right, and their congregations have acquiesced in their doing so, then these churches probably deserve what is happening to them today. What is happening may in fact be a form of divine judgment for the enormity of their failure to proclaim the full gospel of Christ in situations where it was easier to debate the relative merits of sheep and cow manure for rose gardens or hold consecration services, followed by afternoon teas, for red horsehair couches.

A thoughtful, committed minister today has a shining opportunity to preach the gospel in a world where the old systems and values are falling into ruin, thus magnifying the needs of the people for leaders and reliable voices. The situation is not unlike that enjoyed by Chrysostom, of preaching to the people of Constantinople while they waited with bated breath for news of what the emperor might do to their city for some youths' having desecrated the royal statues; or by Augustine, whose treatise on the City of God provided theological comfort in the years when Rome was visibly decaying from the inside and yielding to the onslaught of the barbarians on the outside; or by Martin Luther, whose discernment of a new way of being religious appeared heaven-sent to many who were wrestling with the cultural shift produced by the new spirit of democracy, exploration of the undeveloped territories, the discovery of printing, a renaissance of learning, and the rise of a new economic system; or by John Wesley and George Whitefield, who stepped into the breach at a time when industrial machinery was changing the face of nations and creating vast inequities in wealth and power. Lazy spirits will deplore the changes presently occurring, disrupting former theologies and ways of organizing the church. But devoted and inventive pastors will see that this is one of the rare times in history when the Word is able to stir and shape as it did in the time of Christ, so that it becomes a true *Logos*, designing and forming the world in bold new ways consonant with the will of the continuing Creator.

Reaffirming A Sense Of The Transcendent

One of our greatest tasks, in a world that has been so heavily indoctrinated by the Enlightenment and its twin emphases on reason and empiricism, is the refurbishing of our people's faith in the transcendent, the holy, the supernatural, the extraordinary that inhabits the ordinary. The English novelist J.B. Priestley once wrote a novel called *The Flatlanders*, about an unusual race of people who saw everything in only two dimensions. There are many people in our congregations today who might well be enlisted into such a race, for they have been so thoroughly brainwashed by years of education and media treatments of the glories of science that they instinctively label as superstitious anything that has not been subjected to investigation in a laboratory. When I once used the phrase "the Holy" in a manuscript that had gone to the publishers, a young editor "corrected" what I had by inserting the word "Spirit" after it. When I protested to her that I meant the *Holy*, as in transcendence and "the Wholly Other," and not the *Holy Spirit,* she simply responded, "Oh, in that case I don't think anyone will understand what you are talking about."

But it is crucial to our preaching of the gospel, in an age when worlds collide and cultures merge, to lift people's eyes above the mundane nature of global economies, deconstructive philosophies, medical breakthroughs, and electronic modes of communication to the MYSTERY that rises like a vapor from all of them, as though something genuinely sacred were being released in the ongoing process of creation, as though we approached, in all our explorations and discoveries and recombinations of life and thought, not some drab, sterile laboratory at the heart of the gray earth but the true SANCTUM SANCTORUM, the HOLY OF HOLIES where we shall stand with heads bowed and eyes averted before the AWESOME POWER of a LOVING AND CREATIVE GOD.

Annie Dillard had the size of it when she wrote *Teaching a Stone to Talk.* She said:

> On the whole, I do not find Christians, outside of the catacombs, sufficiently sensible of conditions. Does anyone have the foggiest idea what sort of power we so blithely invoke? Or, as I suspect, does no one believe a word of it? The churches are children playing on the floor with their chemistry sets, mixing up a batch of TNT to kill a Sunday morning. It is madness to wear ladies' straw hats and velvet hats to church; we should all be wearing crash helmets. Ushers should issue life preservers and signal flares; they should lash us to our pews. For the sleeping god may wake someday and take offense, or the waking god may draw us out to where we can never return.[3]

How do we go about reintroducing the notion of the transcendent in a world of flatlanders? James Wall, editor of the *Christian Century,* has suggested that one way is to point to the movies people watch, and especially the ones they have enjoyed because they contained glimpses of the beyond, as in the supernaturalism of *Field of Dreams*, with the old-time ballplayers coming out of the cornfield, or *Ghost*, in which a young man who has been killed lingers near his sweetheart to protect her from gangsters seeking to terminate her life. There is a similar recognition of transcendence, says Wall, in the Danish film *Babette's Feast,* at the moment when the old general stands to make a speech after the wonderful meal he has eaten, and realizes that all life is held together and unified by the grace of a God who asks only that we accept it.[4]

Wall's comments prompt us to remember that the cultural mode our age is moving into is one that supports electronic images instead of linear description. It may well be that after having lost the sense of the Holy in an age of print and linear description we shall now discover it again in the world of images. F. W. Dillistone has said in *Religion and Symbolism* that the modern world is almost totally bereft of the kind of redemptive symbols that once mediated meaning and spirit to people — symbols such as water, wine, bread, cross — and that is impossible to reproduce them by artificial means. This is true, as little as we wish to admit it. Many modern congregations have even repudiated the classic Christian symbols as no longer speaking to them. But if there is any correlation between the symbol-creating powers of people in the preliterate age and those of people in the postliterate age, then there may well be hope that we are on the verge of a much richer age, imagistically and symbolically, than we have yet experienced.

There may also be a clue in this discussion to the impetus, in recent years, for preaching through narrative, myth, and parable. Some of us, born below the Mason-Dixon line, have frankly been amused at the enthusiasm displayed by many seminary professors for the genre of narrative preaching, which they seem to believe they have invented, because we grew up under the ministries of pastors who didn't know how to preach in any other way. But it is probably true that people nurtured on electronic screens and images find sermons with stories and verbal images more compelling than old-fashioned doctrinal sermons filled with argument and exhortation. They learn and apprehend truth more through images and illustrations than through propositional speech. It may therefore be possible, as Wall suggests, to cultivate a new feeling for the transcendent by merely pointing out the places where it seems to appear in the extraecclesial, secular world.

The movie *Grand Canyon* is a case in point. Set primarily in Los Angeles, the movie opens with a chilling scene in which a spectator leaving a Lakers ballgame at night has to call a wrecker when his car stalls on a back street. Four armed hoodlums approach as he waits for the wrecker and demand that he get out of the car. As the terror mounts, the wrecker arrives. The driver orders the owner of the car into the cab of his truck, quietly faces down the hoodlums, and tows the car to an all-night garage. The two men, one white and one black, become friends, and some wonderful things happen as a result of the friendship. Later, when the white man's wife has discovered an abandoned Hispanic baby under some bushes in the park and her husband doesn't think they should adopt it, she reminds him of his meeting with the wrecker driver and talks about the ''miracles'' that happen all the time in our lives that we are too insensitive to see. Indeed, the whole movie is about such miracles, and, at the end, the wrecker driver takes the white family, his nephew, and his girl friend to the Grand Canyon, which stands as a kind of elemental monument to the presence of the miraculous in the world.

There isn't any talk about God in all of this. The people in the movie are extremely secular. When they do refer to the fact that they live in ''the city of the angels,'' it is with a hint of irony or sarcasm. They work in secular environments; they speak with the profane language of secular people; they don't go to church. But they do flirt with the possibility that there is something transcendent in our midst that we don't normally recognize or know about. And it would be an easy step, in a sermon, to identify this transcendence for audiences that have seen the film, and to remind them that this is what the biblical faith is all about, in its nakedest, most elemental form. The very world we live in is a miracle of God, and that is why Jesus came to teach us to celebrate it and share it and accept it as a sign of divine love.

The film makes a point that we ought to make in all our sermons, that the transcendent is not something that overwhelms us with otherness, transporting us out of the world of everydayness, but, on the contrary, is something present in the ordinary stuff and relationships of our common lives, something we need only a little training to see. The lesson of the Incarnation is that God has visited us in Christ, in muscle and bone and sinew, in eyes and nose and sweat and hair, in feet that become caked with dust and hands that are thick and calloused by labor. If the impact of this were ever truly registered among us, we might indeed wear crash helmets in church and ask to be lashed to our pews.

What we seek, in the end, is not to turn our parishioners into otherworldly persons, ethereal wraiths dancing on the cusp of the world, but to deliver them more solidly than ever to the real world they live in. We want them to sense the holiness in bread and wine, the miracle of families and friendships, the specialness of everything that is. Then they will value other persons, treasure the environment, revere the potential in children, and celebrate the rule of God wherever it is coming in the world.

There is a beautiful illustration of this desideratum in H. A. Williams' autobiography, *Some Day I'll Find You*. Williams, an Anglican priest, was captivated by the idea of ministry after hearing William Temple preach at St. Mary's in Oxford. The sight of an archbishop in all his robes "uttering a ceaseless stream of words in a rotund style and fruity voice" totally mesmerized him, and he vowed to become a priest for the glamor in it. After assignment to his first parish in London, he began to feel deep waves of guilt because of his inclination to homosexuality, and the growing tensions in his life precluded his really seeing the holiness of God around him.

One winter's afternoon shortly after World War II, when fuel was still scarce, Williams thought he would get warm by taking a brisk walk in Regent's Park. It was nearly tea time and the sun was beginning to set. A snow had just fallen, imposing a deep quiet on the park. But Williams must tell of it in his own lovely voice:

> *The trees with their leafless branches thinly covered with snow looked like the ethereal guardians of some sublime secret. The grass was white with patches of green here and there as though it rejoiced in the snow without being overwhelmed by it. The shrubs were bursting through their white covering as if delightedly playing a game. And the sun — a combination now of gold and red — suffused the air and gave its colour to everything. It was impossible to conceive of anything more glorious than what lay around me. It was overpowering without losing any of its gentleness. It was blessedness and love.*
>
> *Or it should have been. But it wasn't.*[5]

It wasn't, because Williams was at that time incapable of perceiving the transcendent. Or, if he did perceive it, he perceived it only in terms of an anguish that lay heavily in his heart, a sense of despair that seemed to blind him to the glory around him. He was, in short, very much like all the secularized folks in our congregations, who see only the surface of life and the world, and miss the glory of them.

Later, Williams suffered a complete breakdown. He arrived at a point where he could not even get out of bed and move across his room. Years of attention from a caring therapist were required to restore him to normal functioning and feelings of personal adequacy. But at the end of this journey, which he would remember as truly a "sacred journey," his healing was so complete that he not only regarded the world normally, he regarded it even better than normally, he saw it as "the encompassing mystery of God," a great sacrament mediating the divine to human beings.

He cites two evidences of this better-than-normal viewpoint. One occurred when he was on a business trip to Trinidad and made the journey from San Fernando to Port of Spain on an ancient, dilapidated bus. During the two-hour journey he became so caught up in a sense of bliss, with an experience of the ultimate reconciliation of all things "as Love, a living presence," flooding over him, that he quite forgot where he was and did not notice when the bus arrived at Port of Spain. When he did not descend with the other passengers, the conductor tapped him lightly on the shoulder and asked if he was all right. He then saw that the bus was empty, thanked the conductor, and got off. But he was so transported by the experience that he walked around the city for half an hour, just recovering from what he had felt, before going to his meeting.[6]

Another time, Williams entered a crowded cateferia at Waterloo Station and had the overpowering feeling that the place was the biblical village of Emmaus, where Christ broke bread with his disciples. As he looked over the crowd, he had the unmistakable sensation that the tea and buns they were consuming were the holy sacrament, and that the divine presence was once more breaking through to speak to him — indeed, to all of them — in the midst of the ordinary.[7]

These are hardly the delusions of a man who has experienced a breakdown and is therefore prone to seeing reality a little less accurately than others. On the contrary, Williams went on to become one of the acutest minds of the Church of England, and a widely respected theologian and preacher. No, the truth of the matter is that these are the kinds of experience of the Holy in our midst that we all should be fortunate enough to have from time to time, and would, if we only practiced more assiduously the art of beholding transcendence.

They beautifully illustrate the sort of oneness of vision we hope to instill in our parishioners, so that they too, while living a modern, secular existence, never fail to see through the veil of everyday experiences the sure presence of the deity converting the crass materiality of this world into the energy and spirit of the world that has been promised.

Preaching Christ

After years as a pastor and preacher and itinerating speaker, I have to say that it is my experience that the best way to remind people of the Holy, to reintroduce them to the transcendent in the midst of the mundane, is merely to begin talking about Jesus.

Not piously.

Not esoterically.

Not proprietarily.

But simply, casually, honestly, sincerely.

Paul the Apostle discovered this in his great sweeping evangelistic tours. He was smart enough, by the time he got to Corinth, that bustling, cosmopolitan city sitting astride the isthmus between mainland Greece and the Peloponnesus, not to rest his case in rabbinical arguments or philosophical sophistries, although both would probably have appealed to his hearers there. What he had discovered again and again, as he traveled from city to small town to countryside, was the sheer power of simply talking about Jesus and his death on a cross.

It was as uncomplicated as that.

He went into a town and asked directions to the synagogue. He went into the synagogue, joined in the prayers, listened to the readings, and began talking about Jesus, and how his remarkable ministry — no, his remarkable *person* — was the summation of everything promised in the scriptures. And immediately he would sense the power in the room, the awesome presence, the spirit of something beyond all human reason.

It seemed to produce a kind of cataclysm. Some people would be drawn at once to this new teaching. Others would become agitated, angry, mysteriously repelled by it. A strange kind of energy would grip the entire populace. Everyone would talk about what was happening.

So Paul, reflecting in a letter to the Corinthians on the manner in which he approached them with the gospel, said:

> *When I came to you, brethren, I did not come proclaiming to you the testimony of God in lofty words or wisdom. For I decided to know nothing among you except Jesus Christ and him crucified. And I was with you in weakness and in much fear and trembling; and my speech and my message were not in plausible words of wisdom, but in demonstration of the Spirit and of power, that your faith might not rest in the wisdom of men but in the power of God.* (1 Corinthians 2:1-5)

Reading these words again, I remember the occasion when Father Joseph Girzone, author of the famous *Joshua* novels, came to our campus at Samford University to participate in a week-long festival of Christ and the arts. He was the first speaker in a roster that included such illustrious lecturers as Wendell Berry, the poet and essayist, James Wall, editor of *Christian Century,* Vicki Covington, the novelist, and Leonard Sweet, the theologian and historian. Such a pivotal role might well have induced a speaker to work hard at introducing an agenda of important thoughts for the week or displaying personal erudition and brilliance to secure his own place in the admiration of the audience.

But Father Girzone did neither.

He walked out into a crowded auditorium, where people stood three and four deep in the rear, and began talking very quietly about Jesus. He spoke of Jesus' care for the people, Jesus' simple manner of speaking, Jesus' way of cutting through hypocrisy, Jesus' unswerving devotion to God, Jesus' joy in living, Jesus' extraordinary transparency to his Father. Jesus, Jesus, Jesus. He didn't talk about anything else. For an hour and fifteen minutes, he talked about Jesus, and not a person stirred or coughed or became restless, and not a soul left the auditorium before he had finished, even though many were late for classes and appointments elsewhere.

It was a remarkable experience. There was absolutely nothing new in what Father Girzone said. It had all been told a thousand million times. There was nothing new about *how* he said it. His speech was simple, direct, without embellishment. And yet everyone said afterwards that it was one of the highlights of their lives, that something miraculous had happened in that auditorium, that you could feel the presence living and breathing there.

I thought about all the sermons I have labored over in my preaching lifetime. Hundreds and hundreds, perhaps thousands of meticulously crafted pieces of communication, each designed to seize the listeners' attention, provoke an important thought, wrestle with it in the listeners' minds as well as my own, and bring it effectively to some challenge for a changed loyalty or renewed commitment.

I thought about my stacks and stacks of preacher's notebooks, with the jottings and scribblings of half a lifetime of reading, listening, observing, and ruminating. All those catchy phrases, arresting titles, deft movements. All the illustrations, culled from libraries, theaters, art galleries, newspapers, conversations, literally almost everywhere I've been and everything I've done. All the references to Bible studies, theological dictionaries, and books of history, theology, anthropology, and culture.

And I remembered Sarah Hickson.

Sarah was a librarian in Lynchburg, Virginia, where I was a pastor for six years. She was one of my parishioners. She was a very unusual woman. Although one would not know it to look at her, she had an unusual physical problem. She inherited from her mother, who died at an early age, a complicated problem with her heart valves. She also had a unique blood type. Researchers for years sought a compatible blood somewhere in the world so that Sarah could have an operation and not die young, as her mother did, but they were unsuccessful. So Sarah, brilliant, well educated, widely read, fascinatingly articulate, lived facing her mortality with a consciousness few of us have, and it made her very wise and deep.

We used to have some wonderful conversations. They always left me exhilarated, high, excited, my mind scrambling from one thing to another.

When I was about to leave Lynchburg, Sarah came to see me in my office. We had a long talk. In the course of it, Sarah touched on my ministry in Lynchburg. She had one piece of advice:

"Talk about Jesus," she said. "Concentrate on him. When you talk about Jesus, something happens. It is special. There are many wonderful things to talk about, and you do most of them well. But when you talk about Jesus, none of the rest seems important. Talk about him."

I haven't forgotten, Sarah. Father Girzone reminded me.

It is true that we live in a very pluralistic and syncretistic time, and that it is important that we behave respectfully toward people of other faiths and lifestyles, cherishing the expanded vision of God their beliefs afford. Nothing ever hurt or offended me more as pastor of a Christian church than to see members of my flock acting in an exclusive or unfriendly manner toward persons of another background. Such behavior usually betokens a closed, uninquiring mind and a narrow, unwelcoming heart.

But this is no reason not to speak about Jesus with enormous respect and enthusiasm.

As Harvey Cox contends in *Many Mansions,* it is the particularities of the various faiths that make dialogue among their adherents truly possible. As soon as participants in an interfaith dialogue stop talking about "my" faith in Jesus or "my" devotion to Krishna and begin to drift into high-level, abstract discussions of doctrine and philosophy, people begin to yawn and look at their watches. Christians should not try to soft-pedal the figure of Jesus himself when dealing with people

of other faiths. "I have noticed," says Cox, "that when reference to Jesus is postponed or downplayed, conversations between Christians and people of other traditions tend to become
arid, but when the figure of Jesus is brought to the fore, either
by the Christians or — as sometimes happens — by the others,
the dialogue becomes alive."[8]

E. Stanley Jones, the great Methodist missionary to India,
had the same experience. In his famous Round Table Conferences that were held in many of the towns and villages of India, he always encouraged the Buddhist and Hindu
participants, who usually numbered about two-thirds of those
present, to testify as fully for their faiths as possible; and he
urged the Christians, who constituted the other one-third, to
do likewise. He did not permit summing-ups, lest those presenting the closing speeches offend anyone by twisting the facts
or putting an unwarranted spin on what had gone before. He
wanted the testimonies to speak for themselves. Jones was always convinced that the Christians had the most powerful arguments, because he knew there was nothing like the gospel
of Christ in the non-Christian world. In all the other religions,
people spoke of working to achieve their form of salvation.
They must laboriously climb the ladder to heaven and hope
to meet God on the topmost rung — if they could get there!
But the God of Christians has come to us, in the Incarnation,
and, instead of meeting us at the topmost rung of our worthiness, has met us at the bottommost rung, where we are sinners. Our redemption is nothing we have done; it is a gift of
God.[9]

This was the constant message of Jesus. Day in and day
out, he reminded the Pharisees and Sadducees that God is no
respecter of persons, that God loves the leper and the tax col-
lector as much as the most respectable members of the community, and that God's table is a festal board precisely because
nobody is worthy to be there and yet everybody is invited.

What Jesus did and didn't say is another matter that gives
some ministers pause about preaching Christ. Suppose Jesus
didn't say all those things; they wonder; maybe he wasn't

everything we think he was; maybe his messiahship is something largely concocted by the early church. If that is true, why should we add to the superstitiousness of the ages by always talking about him? Why not acknowledge that he was probably a good man and mention him with Confucius and St. Francis and Abraham Lincoln and try merely to inculcate a spirit of goodness and decency in folks?

I follow the proceedings of the Jesus Seminar because many of the scholars working on its project are old friends of mine. What the seminar is in the business of doing is deciding by scholarly debate and then by actual vote which of the Gospel sayings attributed to Jesus were actually his words, which were possibly his words, and which were in all probability put in his mouth by the early Christian authors. The members of the seminar have already published a compilation of the four Gospels plus the Gospel of Thomas, with the print in different colors to indicate their judgments about which words originally came from Jesus and which didn't.

I find all of this interesting, at times even fascinating. I have no doubt that some of the sayings were scribal additions, and that, even before that, some were added to the oral traditions by well-meaning persons who couldn't forbear "improving" on the words of the Master. But as far as I am able to tell, it doesn't affect my faith one iota if fully three-quarters of the speech attributed to Jesus is thought not to be his at all. If Jesus had uttered no more than the Lord's Prayer, or even two-thirds of it (the Jesus Seminar has doubts about part of it), or if he had spoken no more than the parable of the Leaven in the Bread or the Good Samaritan, it would have been enough to convince me of the total congruency between his thought and God's. And if he had been a deaf-mute and uttered nothing at all in his entire lifetime, but had laid his healing hands on a single leper or opened his arms to a single outcast or directed a single smile at the poor woman casting her two small coins into the treasury, it would have been enough to assure me that God was somehow in this wonderful man, revealing the kind of antistructures that would one day replace the reprehensible structures and powers of this present world.

There was something so compelling and *right* about Jesus that people in any age can recognize it and will identify with it, will seize upon it and upon him, if we will only preach him and give them a chance to understand who he was and what he stood for as he walked around Galilee and Judea, stirring up life wherever he went. Never mind that this is the eve of the twenty-first century, two millennia after the Christian movement began. Never mind that we live in glass-and-concrete canyons with the ever-present roar of traffic and fumes of gasoline, where people barter their time at computers and fax machines to receive pieces of paper that they take to their banks and that then entitle them to put little plastic cards into impersonal machines, punch in a few numbers, and draw out the cash they use to purchase shoes from Italy, suits and dresses from the Orient, recordings from Nashville, and television sets from Mexico. The man Jesus still speaks so powerfully to the modern mind that an endless stream of sermons, books, and movies doesn't begin to do him justice or exhaust his popularity with the people.

The film *Jesus of Montreal* is a good example. It is about a young actor/director recruited by a Roman Catholic institution to revise the institution's annual, somewhat vapid version of the Passion Play. The actor/director takes his charge seriously and studies and reads copiously in preparation for rewriting the play. Then he goes around recruiting people for the various parts. The play is fresh and compelling, because it really captures the spirit of the gospels and the way Jesus was. Word spreads through the city and crowds of people come to the drama. The church officials become uneasy, because the Jesus portrayed in the play is so anti-institutional that they fear repercussions against the diocese. They try to pull the play, but the actors don't want to stop. They have begun to identify their parts with the holy mission of Christ.

I will not spoil the film by describing the denouement, but the power is still there. For both the audiences inside the film, who come to see the Passion Play, and for those outside it, who have come to see the movie, Jesus is still a "good draw." He still attracts followers, still generates excitement, still acts as a catalyst for the separation of good and evil. He is still the Christ who, lifted up, draws all people to himself. And, if we are to pretend to any kind of ministry at all in his name, then we must preach him, must set him at the heart and center of our sermons and our liturgies, must allow him still to create the community of faith in the midst of a secularized, pluralistic world.

I said that Paul the Apostle recognized the importance of preaching Christ in a similarly pluralistic, syncretistic world nearly 2,000 years ago. This was recently brought home to me again in an almost mystical experience as I was listening to a lecture by Kenneth E. Bailey, an Episcopalian Bible scholar who has lived most of his life in the Middle East and presently teaches in Jerusalem and Tantur. The lecture was about Paul's structuring of his discourse in 1 Corinthians. Specifically, it dealt with the principle of "inversion" or "chiasmus," by which an author, instead of proceeding systematically straightforward in a speech or essay, develops his or her thought in an enveloping pattern, placing the kernel or central idea in the middle of the material, not at the beginning or end. Thus, to put it very simply, the author might develop a proposition according to the diagram C-B-A-B-C, as opposed to A-B-C or C-B-A. We have been accustomed to reading Paul according to a straight sequential pattern, verse after verse, as our modern manner is. But if we really want to understand him, said Bailey, it is necessary to approach the text through the form *he* is using.

As Bailey was explaining this, my eyes were racing ahead to reexamine the first 16 verses of chapter one of 1 Corinthians. It was true! The chiastic pattern was there. The section began, "Paul, called by the will of God to be an apostle of Christ Jesus" (verse 1) and ended "Was Paul crucified for you? Or were you baptized in the name of Paul? ..." (verses 13-16). Then, from both ends of the section, it worked back toward the middle, where Paul stated the theme of the entire book.

I am going to quote verses 4 to 10 as the core of the section. The bold italics are mine. But see what the Apostle was writing:

4) *I give thanks to God always for you*
because of the grace of God
which was given you in **Christ Jesus,**

5) *that in every way you were enriched in him*
with all speech and all knowledge

6) *— even as the testimony to* **Christ**
was confirmed among you —

7) *so that you are not lacking in any spiritual gift,*
as you wait for the revealing
of **our Lord Jesus Christ;**

8) *who will sustain you to the end,*
guiltless in the day of **our Lord Jesus Christ.**

9) *God is faithful,*
by whom you were called into the fellowship
of his Son, **Jesus Christ our Lord.**

10) *I appeal to you, brethren,*
by the name of **our Lord Jesus Christ,**
that all of you agree
and that there be no dissensions among you,
but that you be united
in the same mind and the same judgment.

The name of our Lord Jesus Christ is like the fusillade of a mighty cannon sounding from the walls of some invincible battlement. *Boom, boom, boom,* it sounds, reverberating through everything along its path. Was the Corinthian church in difficulty? Let it remember Christ! Were the people at odds with each other? Let them remember Christ! Were they having difficulty with immorality? Let them remember Christ! Were they disputing about doctrine and party? Let them remember Christ!

Christ, Christ, Christ, Christ.

It struck me with the force of an overwhelming emotion: The only reason our churches are in trouble is that we have gotten away from Christ. It was so simple I wanted to laugh and cry at the same time. I felt happily blown away. I wanted to dance and shout. I wanted to say, "This is it! If we will only learn to talk about Christ again, to live in the presence again, we will survive the culture shift, our churches will find their way once more, it will all be fine."

I know it isn't easy. We live in a tough and complex world.

But this has *got* to be the key.

Exalting The Rule Of God

Transcendence and Christ.

It is all about the rule of God, the divine moment when the world as God envisions it begins to break through the crust of the world as we know it, detonating the old world and the old regimes and the old structures, sending them flying into outer darkness like fragments of debris from an exploded shell or bits of dry cocoon sloughed off by a glorious butterfly.

For those with eyes to see and ears to hear, it is already happening. The strains on the old structures are becoming daily more visible and audible. They are groaning and splitting, beginning to give way to the new age.

We used to sing "The kingdom is coming," before this era or greater sensibility, which is also a sign of the birthing of the new. Now, out of respect for the feminine in society, and its equality in God's eyes, its tender, dancing, nursing presence, we speak of the "rule" or "reign" of God, the full arrival of divine ascendancy, when lion and lamb lie down in peace and male and female achieve the dreamed-of blessedness they remember from the Garden of Eden. James Fowler in *Weaving the New Creation* calls it the "Commonwealth of Love and Justice."[10]

It is this commonwealth of God we should be pointing to in our preaching, not the church.

The church is an excrescence of the rule of God, not the other way around. We tend, in our natural imperialism, to forget this. We find it easy to believe that the order of revelation is GOD-CHURCH-WORLD, when in fact, as J. C. Hoekendijk has reminded us, it is, has always been, GOD-WORLD-CHURCH.[11] God so loved the world, not the church. God's beauty and creation are seen in the world, not the church. Our problem is that we live and work so long and devotedly inside the church that we get to thinking "church" instead of "world," and start seeing all human existence through stained-glass windows. Just as the old Jews began to glorify the law and the temple until they filled all the space there was, leaving no room for prostitutes and publicans, we glorify the church and the Christian tradition, and forget that they were born to be *servants* of the rule of God, midwives to its birth, not proprietors and directors of everything.

It is no wonder that church members are upset today at the news of the institution's decline and at the sense that nothing is what it used to be. We are all like the besieged king in Eugene Ionesco's *Exit the King,* a play in which news comes in from every quarter of the kingdom that people are dying, the ecosystem is drying up, and everything is disappearing; even the castle walls crack and begin to crumble as the play proceeds, and the king is finally left alone on this throne, visibly shaken and aged and expiring.

But the reason we despair at the dwindling of the institution is that we have lost sight of the movement, the spirit, and have forgotten that the church does not exist and never has existed for its own sake. When we begin to point people beyond the debacle of institutional Christianity in our time to the glorious power of God unleashed in the world, we shall all take heart again and the church will begin to be formed anew, as the community of the faithful, awestricken ones called to witness to the divine message.

As Stanley Hauerwas and William H. Willimon say in *Resident Aliens,* "The overriding political task of the church is to be the community of the cross."[12] We have forgotten this, and have tried to live as the church triumphant. We took the picture of the church at the end of the book of Revelation, when evil has been destroyed and the divine rule vindicated for all the ages, and sought to assume that pose before the time for doing it. Now we must eat humble pie and become again the church we were called to be, the servant church, the church of the cross, the church without status in the world, and live and work and preach from that position, not the other. We must doff the gold vestments and wear the hair shirt again. Then we shall once more see the glory and power of God in the world and learn to live doxologically, not despairingly, and exultantly, not complainingly.

The church will always struggle with prejudice among its members. The rule of God rises above all divisions and inequalities.

The church will always become territorial, speaking of "ours" and "theirs." The rule of God rises above all selfishness, all boundaries, and all parochialism.

The church will always have problems with legalism and Phariseeism. The rule of God is centered in grace and love and freedom.

The church will always be earthbound, limited, and misguided. The rule of God is transcendent and illimitable.

The church will always be fragile and destructible. The rule of God is forever and forever.

I remember Paul E. Scherer's speaking somewhere of a pastoral scene in France during World War One. Evening was falling over the landscape when a German shell whistled through the air and struck the tower of the village church, blowing it into a million pieces. The birds in the area, that had already nested down for the evening, flew instinctively into the air as the sound of the whistle approached; and, when the debris had settled after the explosion, they returned to earth again, as quiet as if nothing had happened.

So it is with the rule of God. It goes on and on, regardless of how many church towers are destroyed or how many denominations rise and fall.

E. Stanley Jones wrote in *A Song of Ascents* that he experienced the transforming truth of this once when he was visiting Russia. He had been depressed by the cold aura of communism in the land, and needed reassurance as he sat in his hotel in Moscow. Then a verse of scripture leapt out at him: "Therefore let us be grateful for receiving a kingdom that cannot be shaken" (Hebrews 12:28). He moved his lips, repeating the words: "a kingdom that cannot be shaken." Not only a kingdom that will not be shaken, he thought, but a kingdom that *cannot* be shaken.

"I saw as in a flash," he said, "that all man-made kingdoms are shakable. The kingdom of communism is shakable: they have to hold it together by purges, by force; they cannot relax that force or it will fall apart. The kingdom of capitalism is shakable. The daily fluctuations in the stock market, on account of the course of events, shows that the kingdom of capitalism is shakable. The kingdom of self is shakable. Center yourself on yourself as the center of your kingdom and the self will sour and go to pieces. The kingdom of health is shakable. The radio and television blare constantly with supposed health remedies to hold this physical life together, but in the end the grim reaper death gets us all. Everything is shakable, except one — the Kingdom of God, the one and only unshakable Kingdom."[13]

This, in an age of global upheaval, of almost catastrophic losses and reversals, is what we must preach. Not the church, but the rule of God. And, when we do, people will rejoice. They will feel something good down inside them, like a tingle they can identify but not place, and they will begin to understand what the gospel is about.

I felt it myself in church recently. My wife and I were visiting little St. Francis of Assisi Episcopal Church in Pelham, Alabama, where Martin Bell, author of *The Way Of The Wolf* and other books, is the rector. The gospel lection of the day was Luke 13:31-35:

> *At that very hour some Pharisees came, and said to him, "Get away from here, for Herod wants to kill you." And he said to them, "Go and tell that fox, 'Behold, I cast out demons and perform cures today and tomorrow, and the third day I finish my course ...'"*

The point of the text, said Martin, in his very precise, very dramatic way, is very simple: Herod doesn't set the agenda, God does. And the sermon was an elaboration of that statement. Herod, Satan, the world, is always trying to set the agenda for us, in terms of trends, social pressures, the expectancies of friends and family; but when we have entered the rule of God we no longer have to pay any attention to that agenda, the only agenda we have to be concerned about is God's agenda. When we are in Christ, the old structures no longer bind us; they have been overruled by another set of structures in which there are grace and freedom and love.

An example of the new structures had come to his attention during the week, said Martin. A young girl who was a member of his congregation had felt denigrated in her school by a program on drugs which, with its strong Southern Baptist overtones, deprecated the use of real wine in the Episcopal eucharist, suggesting that such usage was debauched and un-Christlike. The girl had asserted her freedom in Christ and her affection for the eucharist by writing a letter to her principal, saying in effect what Jesus said to the Pharisees, Herod doesn't set my agenda, God does.

I have thought about that sermon many times. It comforts me in an age when the earth is shifting around me and the waters roar and are troubled. The culture isn't setting the agenda for my life, and neither is the church.

God is.

Suggesting How The Church Can Be Restructured

Is it possible, having said this, that the church itself can hear such a message? And, if it does, can the church begin to rethink its own *raison d'etre* and mission in the world? Can it learn to be a movement again instead of an institution, a community of the cross instead of a vested power in the society?

It won't be easy. Congregations are often as full of pride and resistance as the people who comprise them. I haven't forgotten the president of the Women's Association who walked out of my sermon at Pentecost, when I said that if the church really listened to the Spirit of God the day might come when someone would suggest deeding its property to the Korean Christians whose growing presence in our section of the city was so much more natural than our own. We are only Christ-like up to a point. That woman was and I am. Something in us resists letting Christ go the whole nine yards in our lives. We want to hold on, stay in charge, retain control.

But what if we could give people a sense of how glorious church would be if only God, not the Christians, were in charge of it?

This is what Joseph Girzone has tried to do in his book *The Shepherd*. *The Shepherd* is the story of Father David Campbell, whose conservative ways and committed churchmanship lead to his being made a bishop in the Roman Catholic Church. But the night of his consecration, he has an experience that changes his life. Spending the night in prayer, he first has a vision of a woman he once directed to leave her common-law husband because they were living in sin; she rails against him and the church while her teenage sons hurl stones at the church building. Startled by this vision, David is tortured by thoughts of how the church's legalism has hurt many of the people Jesus wanted to help. Later the same night, David has a vision of Christ walking through the fields. By the end of his vigil, he has committed himself to bringing his church as much into line with Christ's wishes as he possibly can. His diocese is in for some startling changes!

In the months that follow, David reorganizes his staff much less hierarchically than before, so that everyone has a voice in the governance of the church. He turns many of the business affairs over to church members so that the pastors can spend their time witnessing and ministering. He permits a fellow priest to marry, and assigns him to a small parish where the reaction will be minimal. He encourages the pastors to admit divorced persons to the sacraments. He uses church funds to help local pastors set up new programs that will assist the poor and needy. He turns many of the parish schools over to local industries, creating employment bridges for students who need to work. He travels throughout the diocese, making himself available to the priests and people in small parishes. He reassigns nuns and priests who are not pleasant to people, replacing them with personnel who are. He forges alliances with bishops of the Lutheran, Episcopalian, and United Methodist churches in his area, and they plan to combine their memberships, so that there will be one Christ, one church, and one message in their various churches. In a relatively short time, he revolutionizes the entire program of the church to enable it to reflect the spirit of Jesus, and the people of the area respond by crowding the churches and discovering healing and joy for their lives.

Is such a program a mere fantasy? Are churches too set in their ways to respond to our leadership and become more Christlike? David Campbell, in Girzone's novel, makes powerful enemies and faces the ancient powers of evil as he struggles to bring his diocese under the control of Christ. But maybe the problem is that we have allowed the world to set the agenda for our boards and leaders instead of letting Christ set it. We are Americans, and Americans have always believed in bigness and success. Therefore we have sold our boards and leaders on programs of institutional and financial growth. Many of them have applauded us for this, and proclaimed us superior pastors for helping their organizations to succeed. If we were truly convinced that the churches need to be more Christian, not larger and more prosperous, and we possessed the vision of how they could become that way, couldn't we sell to our congregations the desirability of more Christlike actions and programming? Wouldn't it be possible to design sermons that extolled Christ in and through the church as an organization and cause people to want to follow him in all the dealings of the local parish?

James Fowler, in *Weaving the New Creation,* has published some notes on what a Christlike congregation, which Fowler calls a "public church," or one oriented toward serving the public and not merely existing as an institution, might look like. He calls these "characteristics" of public church; they are derived both from theological reflection and from actual observance of several churches in the Atlanta area.

1. Public church fosters a clear sense of Christian identity and commitment. Its identity derives entirely from Jesus Christ, and calls its members to serious involvement with his teachings and ministry.

2. It manifests a diversity of membership, uniting young and old, rich and poor, male and female, blue collar and white collar, educated and uneducated, and people of many ethnic backgrounds.

3. It consciously prepares and supports members for Christian life and witness in a pluralistic society. It strives, in itself and in them, for "civility" in all dialogue and conflict, allowing for differences of experience and opinion.

4. It balances individual development within the congregation and support for people's vocations to be carried on outside the church, in the various economic, technological, cultural, political, and commercial structures that shape our lives. It encourages both koinonia, *fellowship within the group, and* diakonia, *service outside it.*

5. It strives to achieve a fruitful balance between pastoral and lay leadership, with pastors resourcing the laity in ways that allow them to own programs and not merely serve in them under pastoral initiative.

6. It seeks to offer its witness in publicly visible and intelligible ways, by advertising, campaigning, serving, advocating, lobbying, and, when necessary, even protesting, always with the aim of exalting Christ and his teachings in the public eye.

7. It works at shaping a paideia, *or program of instruction and formation, for children, youth, and new members, and one that consistently helps to form maturer members as well.*[14]

Fowler and his colleague Tom Frank at Emory University have been working with graduate students to identify churches in Atlanta that exemplify the qualities enumerated above, and to allow the realities of life in these particular parishes to interact with the list of characteristics to modify it for future learning. They call their project "The Faith and Practice of the Congregation." As it is an ongoing project, their conclusions at this time are only fragmentary and tentative. Among their conclusions are these: that it takes seven to 15 years to grow a functioning public church; much attention must be paid to nurturing and orientation, especially for new members; there are often vigorous arguments over policy matters, and people must be reminded to treat each other with Christian respect and forgiveness; youth groups are often hard to maintain in such churches, because public churches are usually located in metropolitan areas with a great diversity among the young people and long distances to commute for programs; and such churches usually have abnormally high numbers of members who rank near the top (Individuative-Reflective or beyond) of Fowler's seven-stage measurement of faith development.[15]

I cite Fowler's research and theories at such length because they are indicative of a rich fermentation developing these days around the theme of congregational life and ministry. On the hopeful side, in an era when mainstream churches are reporting negative statistics and experiences within their memberships, there are numerous "experimental" churches all over the country attempting to discover meaningful balances between tradition and innovation. Many of them conform in general to the characteristics Fowler and his colleagues have delineated, and bear witness in their communities to the strongly Christlike natures of their leaders and congregations.

If enough ministers are willing to revision the church for the next century and promote this revisionism in their preaching and teaching, perhaps it will give the mainline churches the kind of impetus they need to salvage something worthwhile out of their presently failing institutions. Sermons consistently emphasizing the judgment of Christ's teachings on all selfish human institutions, pointing to the great ecclesial decisions of the Book of Acts, and stressing the ecclesial and theological insights of the Pauline epistles can help the laity of any congregation to understand the nature of the church that is truly Christian and to seek to become that kind of church themselves. This will not always happen where such preaching occurs, and, good and evil being what they are, there will usually be a contest before either wins over the other. But we are only called to be faithful in our preaching, not to guarantee the results. And it is highly unlikely that new forms of the church will rise phoenix-like out of the ruins of the mainstream congregations unless people catch the vision for them from the sermons of their pastors.

Supporting Christian Morality

Just as the Apostle Paul constantly intertwined matters of ecclesiology and morality in his epistles, it is important that ministers today reconnect belonging to the church with new standards of personal and group behavior. In an ethically rudderless age, when most young people and even adults take their moral cues more from television dramas and sitcoms than from the Bible or Sunday school lessons, we have an obligation to help our parishioners restructure their thinking and acting around certain inviolable Christian precepts. To fail to do so is to abandon them to the moral and ethical confusion that easily characterizes a time of shifting cultural values.

I am not suggesting the return of "Christian" legalism, with belligerent stands of the sort Jerry Falwell and the Moral Majority once took on such issues as abortion and homosexuality, and that the Pro-Lifers continue to take on abortion and many right-wing Christians still take on homosexuality. Such legalism is clearly at odds with the teachings of Jesus, who generally opposed the Pharisees for the way they enslaved people by making Jewish law an object of idolatry. We must never forget that Jesus' words, "The sabbath was made for man, not man for the sabbath," streak like lightning through the dark sky of oppressive legalism; they were the shorthand version of his entire program of human restoration, in which love of God and neighbor were so to reorient people's affections that the rest of the law would become an impotent addendum.

What I am talking about instead is the *real* issues of Christian morality, the ones that come into existence precisely because an individual has given his or her heart to Christ, issues such as justice, honesty, truth, stewardship, fair play, peace, and forgiveness. If the world appears to have jettisoned the Ten Commandments as rubrics for disciplined living, it has certainly not lost interest in these matters, but debates them endlessly in the news media, in movies, and on television talk shows. The mainline church can congratulate itself for the

110

extent to which the subtler and deeper issues of morality (love, justice, stewardship, and so forth) have entered the bloodstream of American public life in the last half-century. While many individual churches failed to pass the litmus tests of courage and integrity during the days of racial integration and the Vietnam war, the church's ethical heritage nevertheless came through with flying colors in the beliefs of young people and the anti-establishment in general. We have come a long way, in the public sector, from Nathaniel Hawthorne's *The Scarlet Letter*, with its portrait of legalistic, unnatural Puritanism, to Mary Gordon's *Final Payments* and its sensitive portrayal of compassion.

In Gordon's novel, a young woman named Isabel Moore has just buried her father after several years of illness, during which she was confined to his bedside. For several months, she flounders, trying to discover what she has the aptitude to do with the remainder of her life. Presently she accepts employment as a social worker, going into homes to check on the welfare of ill and elderly people kept by individuals or families under contract to the social services department. One day she is visiting a Mr. Spenser, an 83-year-old man who lives in bed with his teeth out, reading the *Memoirs of Casanova*. He is very polite, and offers to put his teeth in, but she says he need not. They talk with great ease and candor, for Isabel has been accustomed to conversing for hours with her father.

Mr. Spenser says that most people are kind to the elderly only out of guilt. Isabel asks if he doesn't believe in acts of pure generosity. He responds that he finds the very concept of purity rather "jejune." Isabel says he reminds her of a friend she loves but whom she cannot have because he is married and has a daughter. Mr. Spenser talks with her about love and tells her she is a beautiful woman. She doesn't think she is, but his insistence encourages her, and she thanks him.

As she prepares to leave, he asks a favor.

"Name it," she says.

"Let me see your breasts."

111

At first, Isabel says she can't. He wants to know why. She says merely because they are hers. But then she thinks: What could it hurt? She remembers the woman in *The Brothers Karamazov* who tells a priest she cannot give up an adulterous affair because "it gives him so much pleasure and me so little pain." She locks the door, unbuttons her blouse, loosens and removes her brassiere, and stands there.

Mr. Spenser says nothing. He looks, then closes his eyes.

"You have done me a great kindness," he says. "You have given me what I wanted, not what you thought I wanted, or what you wanted me to want."

Isabel dresses. They shake hands very formally. She unlocks the door and leaves.[16]

Some may find prurience in this passage, but I sense instead a great depth of love and mercy, a recognition of our common humanity, an act of genuine and redemptive compassion. What law is operating here? The law forbidding sexual looseness, voyeurism, and lust? Or is that transcended, in Isabel's case, by the law of kindness and generosity? The latter, I would contend. There is more of the authentic spirit of Jesus in Isabel's act than in all the railing against sensuality and pornography by the Jesse Helmses and James Wildmons, and certainly more than in the stern judgmentalism of the Puritan community that condemned Hester Prynne in Hawthorne's novel.

And it is this higher law, the law of love and understanding, that must be identified and taught from our pulpits in the coming century. The media often understand this better than our churches, and their dramas frequently turn on the contrast between the hypocrisy of "good" Christians and the genuine kindness of instinctively well-dispositioned persons in the secular culture outside the church. The preacher can help to dispel the confusion parishioners feel by more consistently identifying Christ's position over against that of the legalists and by saying no to the Phariseeism that continues to plague the church from generation to generation. Care must be taken not to champion mere hedonism and antinomianism. Jesus said that not a jot or tittle would pass from the law "until all is accomplished," and that no one is to teach people to relax in obedience to it. But he also said that he is the fulfillment of the law and that this carries the law beyond the corrupt legalism it tends to engender and into a new spirit in which the heart triumphs over the law in the very process of observing it (Matthew 5:17-20 ff.). It is this new spirit that we need to identify with Christianity, not the old spirit of carping legalism.

Of course we need to teach about money, power, and sex from our pulpits, and hate, envy, drugs, workaholism, and a lot of other things as well. But in the genuinely Christian parish, these subjects will always be seen in the light of the Incarnation and what it has taught us about life as a whole, so that we do not become entangled in an underbrush of secondary issues, as the Pharisees did, but focus on Christ and the higher consciousness invoked by the gospel. The remarkable thing about Christ, or one of the remarkable things, was that he interacted daily with the scribes and Pharisees and never once permitted them to divert him from the central point of his ministry, that God loves and accepts people regardless of anything they have done and that legalism should never be used by any human being as a way of clubbing or rejecting another human being.

For more than a quarter of a century, I have profited and learned from a little story told by D. T. Niles about a man who was moderator of the Church of Scotland and an official of the World Council of Churches. I thought for years the man's name was John Mackie, but someone recently corrected my memory by insisting that it had to be George Macleod, the founder of the Iona Community. Macleod was traveling with two other men, who happened to be from a very conservative denomination I shall not name, to visit small villages in Greece, with the purpose of checking on the expenditure of World Council funds being sent there. The three of them had driven their Jeep over a nearly impassable road into a tiny community to call on the local Orthodox priest. The priest was overjoyed to welcome them, as he seldom saw a comrade of the cloth. As soon as they had entered his house, therefore, he produced the remnant of a box of Havana cigars he had been rationing since the beginning of the war and offered them to his guests. Dr. Macleod took one, bit the end off, lit it, and puffed on it, praising its excellent quality. The other two clerics drew themselves up in a posture of offense and said, "No, thank you, we don't smoke."

Realizing he had offended the two men, the priest was eager to make amends. Hastily, he retreated to his wine cellar, returned with a flagon of his choicest wine, and proceeded to offer it to his visitors. Dr. Macleod accepted a glass, sniffed its bouquet, sipped it carefully, praised its exceptional quality, almost too quickly downed the entire glassful, and requested a second. The other clerics, meanwhile, were more offended than ever. "No, thank you," they intoned as one, "we don't drink."

Later, as the three of them clambered into the Jeep and started back up the road, the two legalistic clergy turned on Dr. Macleod with a vengeance. "Dr. Macleod," they shouted over the noise of the engine, "do you mean to tell us that you are the moderator of the Church of Scotland and an official of the World Council of Churches and you both smoke and drink?!" It was more an accusation than a question.

But Dr. Macleod had had quite enough of their mincing, inhospitable attitude. "No, dammit, I don't," he said. "But somebody had to be a Christian!"

We *do* need to offer moral guidelines to the people who belong to our parishes; that is an inseparable part of the gospel we preach. But the guidelines are not a mere accumulation of moral and ethical traditions from our ecclesiastical past. Those traditions are embedded with all manner of inappropriate moralisms that have attached themselves to Christianity at various times in the history of culture. They have become the hairshirt of the Christian experience, the Pharisaic legalism of our inherited situation, and Jesus himself always sits in judgment on them.

What we must offer people is the higher morality of Christ, that focuses not on the misdeeds of sinners but on the images of hope and love mediated to us by the grace of God. We must talk about a world where people respect the environment as part of a sacred trust; where economics takes into generous consideration the smallest and poorest nations as well as the most favored ones; where education and medical aid are the right of all people and not only those who can afford to pay for them; where the old and infirm are valued as highly as the young and powerful, the men and women work together with mutual respect for the worthiness of their gifts, and the color of a person's skin is something to be admired and treasured, not feared or disliked; where the technology of communications is employed to promote love and unity and understanding, not to mislead or sell inferior products or promote selfish interests; where religion itself is a sensitive journey, a thoughtful probing of life and experience, an expedition for discoveries into the heartland of meaning and joy, not a closing of shutters against the world and its wonders or people and their ways.

Our faith, at its highest, offers people a model and opportunity for sacrificing themselves, for becoming, in Luther's term for it, "little Christs" in the world. There are two respects in which Christianity is unique among the world's religions. One is its insistence that salvation is by grace and not by anything we are able to do for ourselves. The other is the flipside of this, that the minute we have been overcome by grace, and realize our inestimable indebtedness to God, we are led to a spirit of great humility and service, in which we desire to give everything we have into a common storehouse of life and possessions so that the poorest of the poor may begin to share more fully in the produce and benefits of the earth.

It is this combined sense of blessedness and bestowal that we wish to inculcate in our people, so that they become fully whole through the systole-diastole movement of receiving and giving that is at the heart of the gospel and the Christian experience. We remind them of the unspeakable love of God that has claimed them in Christ, reorienting their very lives toward love and peace and joy; and of the natural flow that is thus created in their lives, by which their sympathies and gifts begin to travel outward to others, suffusing the environment with evidences of the grace that has visited them.

Leading People To Engagement

Here, at this point, we have reached the very heart and center of what we are trying to do when we preach about Christ and the rule of God. Our ultimate goal as preachers is to instill in our hearers so strong a realization of the love of God, of the outstretched arms of the waiting Father or the bosomy comfort of the doting Mother, that it is an easy step from the feelings they experience about this to the reminder that the natural response to such generous love is to commit themselves to evangelizing the world, to telling others about Christ and his teachings, and working for the fullest possible realization of a Christlike existence in this world. We want them to achieve, in other words, the final level of James Fowler's "stages of faith," the Universalizing stage, where they are so "grounded in a oneness with the power of being or God" that their new visions and commitments "free them for a passionate yet detached spending of the self in love."[17]

But though this is an easy step it is not always taken. We are often guilty of proclaiming the gospel without sounding its passionate demands, without carrying it through to its ultimate consequences for our hearers, their enlistment in the vocation that rightfully belongs to all Christians and not to the clergy alone. Perhaps we are merely overjoyed when people respond to the good news itself, and forget to ply the message further. Perhaps we have misunderstood the theology of lay vocation. Or perhaps we have been fearful of making demands on our church members that will not be fulfilled. Whatever the reason, we have frequently resigned ourselves to a Christian world in which we, the clergy, offer token sacrifices for our congregations and expect too little of the members themselves. I am as guilty as the next one of you. I have labored long and hard at my duties as a minister, often wringing my hands that it made so little difference because no one else was helping and the waves of my influence so quickly died out. But I now realize it was wrong of me to feed my own sense of self-righteousness by allowing myself to be burned out by all there was to do, without regularly sounding the challenge of discipleship to others and insisting that they were missing the greatest delights of the Christian experience by not accepting involvement in the total ministry of the church.

One reason our Protestant system has failed in the continual reforming of itself, which was supposed to be its genius, is that we ministers have failed to exercise our original understanding of the place of the laity in the work of God's commonwealth. We have accepted a *de facto* categorization of the membership of the church, a "heirarchicization," if I may coin an awful word, that has delegated certain fiscal and menial tasks to the laity while denying them a fuller participation in the theological, exegetical, and hermeneutical work of our congregations, which we have reserved mainly for ourselves. We have thus made the laity the guardians of tradition and routine without warrant to change the tradition and routine, and now find ourselves again and again in opposition to them, trying to break into the castle they defend and wrestle ecclesiastical viewpoints into more acceptable contemporary form. Instead of having congregations engaged in constant and lively debate about the meaning of the gospel and how it should be enacted at the local level, we have a gridlock of rules and machinery that can be eased only carefully and slowly if at all.

How daring it would be if we began to preach sermons suggesting that our lay members assume more and more of the responsibility for the church's theology, thus attacking the gap that usually exists between a theologically educated clergy and a theologically ignorant laity. To do this would mean, of course, that we ministers took more pains to point the laity to accessible sources of theological information, did more substantive teaching in our homilies, and provided more class and seminar opportunities where lay people could obtain the kind of understanding they would require for making responsible contributions to congregational discussions. It would also mean surrendering our need to be right and to be visibly in charge of everything; there would be no real partnership if we merely patronized the congregation, reserving the prerogative of vetoing its deliberations and decisions at any point.

But what a joy such congregations could become! Imagine being the pastor of a group of people excited about studying the New Testament, reviewing church history, and becoming conversant in theology in order to take part in meaty congregational discussions about the life and ministry of the people of God. Instead of feeling run over and burned out all the time, such a pastor would feel constantly renewed and reinvigorated, marveling at the grace of the spirit operating in his or her parish. The church would then be like the exciting "learning organizations" being promoted by many modern corporations within their own ranks, that involve *everybody* inside them, not merely the officers and administrators, in systems thinking and ongoing dialogue about how to make the corporations more efficient, humane, and meaningful to society. (For a lengthy but excellent digest of American business thinking along these lines, I recommend Peter M. Senge, *The Fifth Discipline: The Art and Practice of the Learning Organization*.[18] Senge even speaks at one point of the *metanoia* [the New Testament word for "conversion"] necessary to shift stodgy old corporations into the vital new mode that can save American businesses.)

One of the reasons people in an age of massive culture shift like ours have difficulty making commitments is that they are faced with so many options that they don't really know what to commit to. They lack the ability to process the reams and reams of data coming to them every day and arrive at meaningful decisions about how to arrange their priorities and live their lives. They tend to reserve themselves, floating above the possibilities, until they can achieve more clarity, or else are forced into positions by events themselves. Many of them become so practiced at this position of "permanent reservation" that they become quite incapable of taking definitive action about anything, their jobs, their housing, their marriages, their retirements, even their vacations. The editorial boards of magazines, sensing this extreme tentativeness, often focus articles on "the best hotels," "the best travel bargains," "the best places to retire," "the best ways to choose a new job," "the best ways to invest your savings," "the best four-wheelers for the money." We simply live at a time when the plethora of choices can be paralyzing and destructive.

What we can do for our parishioners with our preaching, therefore, is a service they will find nowhere else. We can help them to become committed to what Fowler calls "a shared master story" or "core story"[19] that we believe is essential to the life God intends for the world. We don't have to spell out all the ramifications of the story — that would spoil it for them and their development as responsible Christians — but we do need to identify it clearly and regularly for them, so that it becomes the inescapable presence in our liturgical services, board and committee meetings, and times of fellowship. And then we need to urge upon them the importance of their becoming involved with the story, of narrating their own stories and discerning how they interweave with *the* story, and then of finding ways to conform the future narrative line of their stories with that of *the* story, so that it enjoys both the security of being anchored in timeless myth and the freedom of discovering its own adventure with *the* story.

I don't mean that we must become obnoxiously evangelical, bludgeoning people into the household of God and then handing them preprinted directives about how they are to conduct themselves as members of the family. I am as nervous as the next person about being in the presence of self-assured Christians who hold the very blueprints for the future pattern of my Christian existence. What I do intend is that, however pleasant and reserved we may be in presenting the "shared master story," like Sir John Gielgud playing the role of a polite high churchman in a sophisticated English country setting, it is important that we leave no doubt in our hearers as to the extreme urgency of their becoming engaged with the story, so that their involvement with its themes may begin to unfold, bringing meaning and redemption to their existence, and doesn't remain merely hypothetical or theoretical.

What we must remember, as preachers, is that this is precisely the task, and none other, that is indicated by our calling to be ministers of the gospel, and it is only in the fulfillment of it that we can justify our ordination and our ongoing relation with a particular congregation. I fear that, in the ever-increasing agenda of parish duties, we do forget this, and permit staff meetings for program planning, committee meetings for everything under the sun, and weddings and funerals and luncheons and dinners and, more and more these days, breakfasts and teas, to siphon off our energies and rather completely divert us from the very thing that originally engaged our devotion to ministry. So it is our salvation, as well as the congregation's, that is at stake in recovering this vital function of preaching. We have not done our jobs until there is in our parishes a rising sense of excitement about what it means to be committed to the narrative of Christ's birth, ministry, death, and resurrection.

We began this book by talking about the disintegration of Protestantism as we have known it, and the anguish and confusion of parishioners and ministers alike concomitant upon that disintegration. Then we discussed the reasons for the disintegration, including the enormous cultural shift occurring worldwide as we approach the end of the twentieth century. We looked at the effect these drastic changes are wreaking in the lives of most of the people who continue to come to our churches and sit in the pews as we preach on Sunday mornings. And finally, in this chapter, we have attempted to review some of the themes and factors that must be present in our preaching if it is to speak with real helpfulness to these souls.

Now imagine what could happen in our churches, decimated and decrepit as many of them are, if we could only secure the primary commitment of the folk remaining with our institutions to a reconsideration of the meaning of the core story and its application to the time in which we live. Does anyone doubt the power of the Holy Spirit to regenerate the church through such an encounter? How many people would need to capture a new vision, in the average broken and wasted congregation, for there to be a rebirth of power and energy in it? A dozen? Half a dozen? Fewer than that?

I remember the story told by D. L. Moody about a frigid English congregation for which he preached one seemingly interminable Sunday morning. The experience was so difficult that he wished he were not slated to return to the church that evening. But everything was different in the evening service. Beginning as a hint of warmth on the face of a single parishioner, it seemed to spread and spread, until the entire congregation was openly receptive and a great revival broke out in the place. Only later did Moody learn the reason. A homebound member of the congregation, an elderly woman, had once read about Moody's great work in America, and had prayed fervently that God would send him to her church to bring the fire of restoration. That Sunday, when her sister had come in at noon and announced that an American evangelist named Moody had spoken in their church, she went without lunch to repair immediately to her room and spend the afternoon in prayer. That one woman, swore Moody, was responsible for the spirit that began moving in the congregation, and for the eventual rekindling of faith in its midst.

Suppose we are quite honest with our congregations, and delineate for them the terrible crisis our churches are in. Surely there is nothing to be gained by trying to conceal the truth until it rises like a spectre to haunt us for not announcing it. In the midst of that awful news, we turn once more to the good news, faithfully reminding people of the transcendence of God, and how it broke in upon us at the Incarnation and has continued ever since to manifest itself where Christ is met and known, the extraordinary inhabiting the ordinary, the spiritual in the midst of the profane. What we can see if we only look rightly, we point out, is the ever-growing rule of God, the commonwealth of heaven, making its way in the very midst of our secularity, punctuating our films and journals and social and political arrangements with reminders of the efficacy of Christ's teachings in the worldly arena. In the light of all this, they should feel the calling to lives of the highest morality, in which the priorities and genuine compassion of Christ triumph over all lesser demands, thus restoring fellowship among God's children, sharing all wealth, education, and technology equally among the peoples of the earth, establishing the sacredness and guaranteeing the protection of the ecosystem, and leading to lives of true spirituality, in which God is ever loved and praised for God's eternally dynamic and ever-growing self. Finally, our people should sense from this cumulative list of emphases the gripping and undeniable importance of their response to it all, their passionate and unreserved embrace of the core story and its implications for their most intimate dreams and plans, their total commitment to the Way of which Christ spoke, that implies not a destination arrived at but the sharing of a journey, the assumption of an adventure that will not only profoundly alter their lives but will mean new life and vigor for the church of Jesus Christ in the next millennium.

Only God knows what a difference we can make!

1. Thomas H. Troeger, *The Parable of Ten Preachers* (Nashville: Abingdon Press, 1992), p. 21.

2. W. H. Auden, *The Age of Anxiety* (New York: Random House, 1947), p. 134.

3. Annie Dillard, *Teaching a Stone to Talk* (New York: Harper and Row, 1982), pp. 40-41.

4. James Wall, lecture, "Movies, Mystery, and Modernity," at Samford University, Birmingham, Alabama, February 26, 1992.

5. H. A. Williams, *Some Day I'll Find You* (London: Collins/Fount Paperbacks, 1984), p. 241.

6. H. A. Williams, *op.cit.,* p. 247.

7. H. A. Williams, *loc.cit.*

8. Harvey Cox, *Many Mansions: A Christian's Encounter With Other Faiths* (Boston: Beacon Press, 1988), p. 6.

9. E. Stanley Jones, *A Song of Ascents* (Nashville: Abingdon Press, 1968), p. 238.

10. James W. Fowler, *Weaving the New Creation: Stages of Faith and the Public Church* (San Francisco: HarperCollins, 1991), p. 142.

11. J. C. Hoekendijk, *The Church Inside Out* (Philadelphia: Westminster Press, 1964), p. 71.

12. Hauerwas and Willimon, *Resident Aliens,* p. 47.

13. Jones, *A Song of Ascents,* pp. 149-150.

14. Fowler, *Weaving the New Creation,* pp. 154-162.

15. Fowler, *op.cit.,* pp. 167-170. For the stages of faith development, see James Fowler, *Stages of Faith* (San Francisco: Harper and Row, 1981).

16. Mary Gordon, *Final Payments* (New York: Ballantine Books, 1978), pp. 205-206.

17. Fowler, *Weaving the New Creation,* p. 113.

18. Peter M. Senge, *The Fifth Discipline: The Art and Practice of the Learning Organization* (New York: Doubleday Currency Books, 1990).

19. Fowler, *Weaving the New Creation,* p. 101.